The Great Compromise

Getting Past the Emotional Nonsense Dividing

America

Daniel Moir

ISBN: **0989525309**
ISBN-13: **978-0989525305 (Epic Odyssey)**

DEDICATION

To Mom and Dad for teaching me everything I know.

CONTENTS

Introduction:

So we survived the end of the Mayan Calendar. However, if you look at the state of our nation, you'd be hard pressed to explain how. Despite what the news media might tell you, the economy is not improving. We are less wealthy than we were as a nation five years ago, and it is a truism we are also less free. We are seeing a government addicted to spending, taxing and banning everything from *Flaming Hot Cheetos,* to sodas over 16 ounces. We are witnessing in abject horror as the President and congress are using class and race as a wedge and bludgeon to divide us, rather than take personal responsibility for their own failings. All the while them media has taken on the role of Ministry of Propaganda for the administration, using it to distract us from the insane spending, and regulations which threaten to collapse this country completely. Meanwhile our cost of living has shot up drastically and our government uses cheap accounting tricks to deny the existence of inflation. Ask yourself this question: is it cheaper now to buy gas, groceries, pay your taxes, upkeep your car, your house, pay your utilities, etcetera, or was it significantly cheaper not all that long ago? Along those lines how does your personal paycheck look? Is it any bigger? How are YOU coping with the crisis that has hit your personal finances? What has the government done to lessen YOUR burden?

Of course if you watch the news all through the 2012 election cycle you'd think the biggest issue facing our nation was that Mitt Romney wanted to take away contraception, that the GOP was waging an insidious war on women, and wanted to deport Latino grandmothers, or wanted to put African Americans back into slavery (per Joe Biden). Never mind that it is a point of historic fact that it was the Democrats who had enslaved the Blacks, and the Republicans who fought to free them, then put in place the 13th and 14th amendment to end slavery... but that's another book. It was a stunning accusation, especially when you consider that all of the famous racists were all Democrats, including Bull Conner, and Sen. Robert Byrd, even Sen. Al Gore Senior... but again, that's another book. Still, one has to wonder how people can accept this premise given the historic reality.

The greatest tragedy facing America is the death of reason in politics. All factions have had a role to play in perpetuating this problem, thus there will be no faction that is safe from my criticism, because I am sick of the politics of distraction. It's not that I aim to offend all, but rather we all made serious mistakes in the 2012 cycle, and I believe that rather than addressing the issues which caused our surprise defeat, we are once again jumping on the distraction issue bandwagon. We are waving around papers about changing demographics, and ignoring the studies that show our near universally nil birthrate, which nullifies any changes to national demographics. We are once again distracted, and we are once again at each other's throats when we ought to be standing together against those who are threatening this country's long term economic health.

By now you are asking what makes me qualified to address these issue? It's a fair question to ask. I am neither pundit, nor politician. I am, for all intents and purposes, a Joe No-One from Nowhere, Utah. However, I have been involved with politics a long time. I had been a student of the Healing of America seminars, sponsored by the Thomas Jefferson Center for Constitutional Restoration. I studied with them for four years prior to joining the UTGOP as a volunteer, six months before the Tea Party entered the equation. I was made into a Precinct Chair for the Murray area, then a Leg Chair and in the 2010 cycle. I was one of but a few boots on the ground, going door to door rather than programing robo-calls. It was a lot of hard work, but at that time we all seemed to want the same thing: to stop the country from continuing the accumulation massive debt.

We were laser focused on fiscal issues in 2010, and had a great deal of success getting Republicans elected back then. Sadly, I had to move to Tooele and haven't been as involved in the political landscape out here, but still remained involved with the Salt Lake County Young Republicans Club, I have a lot of friends there. So by now you know I swing right, or so I'm told. Here's the funny thing, only on fiscal matters and matters of liberty. On social matters I tend to agree with Fox's Greg Gutfield, who in his book *The Joy of Hate* said it best, "I don't care, I don't care, I don't care, I don't care... Stop Tweeting about it!"

I was stunned by how quickly we got off track in 2012; how the synergy of the 2010 cycle was kicked aside in favor of inter-factional fighting over distraction issues like immigration, abortion, gay marriage. Of course the media had you believe that everything that went wrong was that oh-so evil Tea Party's fault, even when the Tea Party didn't have a formal dog in the fight (IE the fight over immigration in Utah). You see some Tea Party groups were led by Libertarians who agree with the "Open Borders" philosophy championed by Ludwig Von Mises, and even Milton Friedman, but that never ended up in the newspapers who saw an opportunity to distract and divide us and took it. The defeat in 2012 was handed to us not by losing a civil debate or changing demographics, but by inter-factional fighting over less important issues, refusal to address the distractions levied by the Democrats, and the fear being promoted by a completely and ridiculously biased media.

It's time for us to end the fear. In this book I will put forward several proposals which some on the Left will love, some on the Right will hate, and vice versa. They are proposals I have come to after years of involvement, study, and contemplation. The fact is that these are things that can be summed up by a simple concept: Let's leave each other alone. Seems easy enough, but the fact is the GOP loves to wag their tongues about what goes on in people's bedrooms, while Democrats can't keep their thieving hands out of other people's pockets, and worse, want people to pay for what goes on in their bedrooms. The simple compromise is: We'll stay out of your bedroom, if you get your grimy paws off my wallet, bank account, and business. Basically, let's everyone mind our own business.

Still with me? Good. This philosophy of *mind your business* seems like the obvious thing to do, yet anyone who promotes it gets booed at Townhalls. My philosophy goes back to that age old Jeffersonian idea that that government which governs best is that which governs least. While I am not an anarchist by any means, we must deal with the fact that Government exists in many areas of our lives it was never meant to be. You call me extreme, I am not. I just like things simple. The simplicity of self-governance is the heart and soul of the modern Conservative-Libertarian-Constitutional-Classical Liberal movement. The simple idea, that we should each be free to govern ourselves, is the winning argument that anyone should be able to get behind, should reason and not emotion prevail.

One should also note that there will be the temptation to call some of these proposals capitulation, but I contend that some of these compromises are merely a political necessity to arrest the leftward swing of the pendulum, hence the cover of this book. I have no intention to lose the war on these issues but we can, should, and must discuss what to do with that pendulum, at a later time, to get it moving back to the real center: the Constitution, and rule by the people rather than a handful of *Harvard* elites. For now, let us examine what must be done to stop it's movement.

Chapter One: Factionalism Is Surprisingly Necessary.

Factions are bad. It's a universal agreement that has been around since the dawn of our country. George Washington's bemoaning of the emergence of factionalism is often cited by the Right, ironically, as evidence that the Two Party system is destroying our country;

> They serve to organize faction, to give it an artificial and extraordinary force; to put, in the place of the delegated will of the nation, the will of a party, often a small but artful and enterprising minority of the community; and, according to the alternate triumphs of different parties, to make the public administration the mirror of the ill-concerted and incongruous projects of faction, rather than the organ of consistent and wholesome plans digested by common counsels, and modified by mutual interests.-1

The funny thing about this is that Washington was indeed annoyed by factionalism, as was John Adams and Alexander Hamilton. Why? Because a little mouse named Thomas Jefferson couldn't keep quiet about the things that that the Washington administration was doing, which he saw as undermining freedom. Jefferson was so upset about some of their positions, he quit his position as Secretary of State and helped to form a new political party... No not the Democrats, that is a misunderstanding that must be corrected. That was Martin van Buren and Andrew Jackson (both of whom Jefferson despised) many years later. No Jefferson would create the Republican Party, or Jeffersonian Republicans, or Democratic Republicans if you prefer. Now hold on a sec, I know that the modern Republican Party traces its roots to Lincoln but there's a reason we've called ourselves GOP, or Gallant *Ole* Party. (Ole=Old for those who may not know.)

Believe it or not, Washington had values and ideals that were more consistent the modern Democratic Party, whom I would argue sprang from the Federalist Party. Washington himself seems non-ideological, he relied heavily on the opinions of Alexander Hamilton for direction. It was this reliance on Hamilton that Jefferson despised. Hamilton didn't want the leviathan government that the modern DNC is fighting for, but he did feel that regulation and debt were needed in order to establish the United States as something of a modern empire of liberty. The Federalists also took a hard line position on the international wars between France and England at the time, and in that moment Jefferson felt we owed the French assistance for their help with our battle with the English a few years earlier. It was Hamilton who advocated the idea of "Friendly relations with all and entangling Alliances with none," a philosophy Jefferson would later adopt, and then abandon when it came time to fight the Barbary Pirates. That was a battle he would wage without congressional approval.

While Jefferson would flip and flop on some of these issues over time, when he formed the original Republican Party, he was fighting for less Federal power and more local power, lower and more uniform taxes, less favors (corporate welfare) for big industry and the promotion of agriculture. He also insisted that welfare and taxation be handled locally rather than federally. Hamilton and Washington, in contrast, were all about a big Federal government, and regulations which tended to favor industrialists over the yeoman farmers Jefferson preferred. Another way of looking at it is that the Federalists favored the city, while Jefferson favored the rural community. Hamilton pushed hard for a large and all-encompassing top down central government, again, not the leviathan we have now. I doubt he could have foreseen the monstrosity his values would lead to, nevertheless if you want to have a civil conversation with a Democrat, (not Occupy Wall Street mind you, real Democrats) one must understand that if you call their ideas Marxist they'll get mad at you. However, if you call their ideas Hamiltonian, the conversation will progress.

There were clear political differences between Jefferson and Hamilton, thus the continuation of one Federalist Party, without opposition, could not continue. Thomas Jefferson and James Madison would organize a formal opposition party, and it was the sudden emergence of resistance to the Hamiltonian Federalists which would lead to Washington's frustrated musings in his farewell address (which was incidentally written by Hamilton, I hear.) Madison, I believe, had a different view on factions and it's one that I share. His writings in Federalist # 10 have been used by both proponents and opponents of factionalism, but as he explores the causes of factionalism one thought emerges: Whether Madison intended Federalist # 10 to read this way or not, he made the argument that factions are necessary to keep one group or another from becoming all powerful and stripping the people, especially minorities, of their liberties. Bi-Partisanship seems to be lending itself to the stripping of individual liberty. Madison may have been intended to show that the US government was never meant to be partisan, but defeated his own argument.

While I agree that partisan bickering can get quite nasty, it is necessary because neither side is one hundred percent right one hundred percent of the time. There are things the Democrats are right about: Corporations are too powerful today, but that is because the government enacts regulations and taxes which keep their competition at bay. What? You thought that Warren Buffet was altruistic? Ha! Warren Buffet has made his fortune he has nothing to fear from higher taxes. Also, notice that he is fighting the IRS right now over a billion dollar bill? The big corporations benefit from big government because the big government gets to select them as the big winners, while enacting crippling rules and regulations which foil any potential competition. Thus assuring the accumulation of wealth into the hands of a very few at the expense of the laborer, who now is unable to get their own business off the ground because of the regulations and taxes of big government. Nevertheless Democrats are right, corporations have too much power, even though they seem disconnected from the cause of it.

Republicans are right about the Federal Government having too much power, even though they supported the Patriot Act, Medicare Part D, the creation of the TSA, DOMA, banning of incandescent light bulbs, TARP, No Child Left Behind and Obama's Common Core, as well as Obama's recent tax increases. It is also worth noting that some of the ideas in Obamacare, such as the Healthcare exchange, and the individual mandate, began as ideas kicked around by Republicans, though to their defense they abandoned those ideas as unconstitutional on their own accord. Still, they are right about the federal government being too powerful, even if they are likewise disconnected from the cause of it.

The two parties only ever seem to notice infringements to our liberty when it is the other party that is the cause, but when they have the chance to undo those infringements they do not. Notice that Obama has only doubled down on the Bush era polices? In 2006 he was part of a Democratic effort to shut down the government over a Debt Ceiling debate. Democrats wanted a repeal of the Bush Tax Cuts, and the shit down was meant to give the Democrats leverage. Obama voted against the final debt deal then, but now calls those on the right who oppose increasing the Debt Ceiling, "reckless and irresponsible." He hasn't really changed the direction we've been moving as much has placed his foot hard on the gas pedal.

All the craziness in Washington is happening because of bi-partisanship. Today partisanship is only a horse and pony show. Notice how Obama demands something, Speaker of the House John Boehner says no, but in the 11 hour

something, Speaker of the House John Boehner says no, but in the 11th hour caves and gives Obama exactly what he wants? How else do we get a tax deal with almost $700 billion in new taxes and only $15 Million in spending cuts, most of which are only cuts from projected spending increases, which have no real weight? This was true in the Bush era as well, notice how few (three I believe) Democrat bills he vetoed from 2006 to 2008, when the Democrats had full control of the House and the Senate? Oh how I long for real partisanship. Those who bemoan it are only upset that someone dares to disagree with them. In a truly partisan environment these encroachments on our liberty would not happen, as one party or the other would do all they can to put a stop to bad legislation. In this regard I have more respect for Obama and his Democrats than I do for John Boehner and his Republicans. Obama is destroying this country, but he has shown his willingness to draw a line in the sand and dare the opposition party to cross it, which they don't. Boehner tends to wet himself, then eagerly put forward a watered down version of what Obama wants, which Obama rejects. Then Boehner wets himself again, retreats to suck his thumb, and then puts forward an even less watered down version of what Obama wanted, which Obama rejects. Boehner then cries himself to sleep, wakes up in a wet bed, then presents a "compromise," which is pretty much what exactly what Obama wanted in the first place, with little, if any concessions for Republicans. If Lincoln handled his battles this way African-Americans would still be in chains.

That is not to say that real compromise cannot be had, that is what this book is about. It does, however, require us to set aside the unimportant issues and focus on the things which are most important. Then we can draw a line in the sand and say, as Jefferson and Madison did in their era, "this far and no further." Both sides need to set aside the nonsense issues, yet both should be willing to take principled stands on issues of liberty and refuse to budge. This book is all about where we need to compromise and where we must not, for in the end Liberty is the only moral argument and nothing else matters.

You might ask yourself what faction am I? I am something of an anathema, something that doesn't really exist anymore. I am something far worse than a Tea Partier, I am a Jeffersonian-Republican. I tend to agree with Jefferson that taxes on consumption is preferable to taxes on income. Taxing both is a double tax and is unfair. Big corporations lead to income disparity and corruption, as the corporations buy power through federal government favors. I do not, however, believe that government has the right to interfere with one's pursuit of wealth. I tend to favor small business and agriculture. I believe in public education but not at the expense of private educators, and not a public education system that doesn't have to compete with private educators. I believe in strong local government and small federal government. While Jefferson would flip and flop between tax uniformity and a progressive tax system, I tend to favor the former. A uniform tax generates more revenue from the rich than it would from the poor by its very nature. However, I acknowledge that taxes should be low and reasonable. The best way to ensure liberty is with a low tax system, which can only be accomplished by limiting the government's power and is best accomplished by eliminating its debt and the projects it takes on that accumulate debt. Like Jefferson, I believe that leaving public debt to future generations is immoral and I also believe there should be no National Bank (Federal Reserve.)

You say, "ah-ha! But then you must be pro-slavery!" Not so, and neither was Jefferson. Yes he had slaves, but he was also an abolitionist. Contradictory? There is no such thing as contradiction, as Ayn Rand would say, "where you find contradiction, check your premise." If Jefferson had had his way, Slavery would have been ended, but it didn't end, in part, because of bi-partisanship.

Let me explain.

When the Federalist Party fell apart, only the Jeffersonian Republicans were left. However, disagreement over direction and issues like Slavery would lead to new factions emerging: the Southern Tertium Quids and the Northern National Republicans. The two would be divided further when John Quincy Adams beat Andrew Jackson in his bid for President. Jackson would go for a round two four years later but as a new party, as a Democrat. The National Republican Party fell into disarray and its moderates would form a new party, the Whigs, which would fall apart after several crushing defeats and the failed presidency of Millard Fillmore.

The Whigs felt compromise was necessary, so you end up with the Mason Dixon line, and the Kansas-Nebraska act, but no end to slavery, only gradual expansion of it. The modern Republican Party didn't emerge until a fringe group of radical extremists lead by Abraham Lincoln began to organize. That new Republican Party came to the rescue with the extreme plan to end the two great barbarisms left in America, polygamy and slavery. A generation passed before we saw Liberty eke out a real victory. Lincoln knew when to compromise and when not to, and he was willing to go to war on the issues he would not compromise on.

Partisanship is a necessary evil. It's annoying, contentious, spiteful... Yet without it Liberty loses every time. Still, there are things we should be able to come together on, as Jefferson would point out, not all disagreements are of principal. In the end we are all Republicans and we are all Democrats.-2 We simply must stop with the bi-partisan agreements that limit our freedom. We have to recognize that there are times when the Democrats are right, and there are times when the Republicans are right and we need to quit insisting on bipartisanship when they are in the right for their lack of it.

Chapter 1 References

1-George Washington, Farewell Address, George Washington, September 17, 1796

2-Derived from Jefferson's 1801 Inaugural Address

Chapter 2: Games, Guns and Both Parties Acting Dumb

Americans are horrified whenever a massive tragedy occurs and rightfully so. We always want to know why, and we always tend to knee jerk react to things. The tendency in America is: "This tragedy occurred therefore liberty must suffer." The Left goes after our guns, the Right blames Hollywood. It never dawns on any of them that the thing that seems to connect these shootings lays underneath the seemingly obvious. Let's be clear, Sandyhook in Connecticut, the Century 16 shootings in Colorado and the shootings in Arizona that wounded a Democratic Congresswoman were all connected by one common factor, all these shooters were paranoid schizophrenics, and as I understand it, all were off their medication.

I must say of the Right, it is depressing to see them go immediately to censorship as the solution, as if the violation of the first amendment will solve the problem when 99.9999% of gamers and movie goers have never gone on shooting sprees. More disturbing is that they jump to this despite the fact that no video games have been positively linked to any of these shootings scientifically. Not a single one of these radio jockeys and talking heads can name a single study which irrefutably links any game to the shootings. Observing that the kids responsible for Columbine played Doom and that Adam Lanza of Sandyhook played Call of Duty is as far as anyone can take it. If these games are the source of the problem, why aren't there millions of Sandyhook incidents perpetuated by the millions of gamers that are out there?

These scare tactics occur despite research by the department of Justice, which shows violent crimes are in decline! A recent guest on the Glenn Beck Program, Colonel David Grossman, went so far as to allege that the mass murderers tend to kill themselves because in the video games that's how you get out of a tough situation. Um… no. Not only does dying in any game in any way set you back, it often results in loss of your inventory advancements, monetary achievements and you may have to start your mission over which is annoying. Also in no game can you point a gun at your own head. Of course, facts don't matter where emotion is running rampant.

There are plenty of games and movies far too violent for my tastes, but they do not allow for intentional suicide. Generally, there is also a distinct good versus evil motif, even in the midst of the violence. Quite seldom does the evil win. Most games are not GTA where you are playing as the bad guy. Most games you are a character like Skyrim's Dovahkin, out to save the world from dragons. In fact, depending on your political views, you are either trying to save the empire from an evil warlord trying to take over the kingdom, or an evil empire oppressing the people (hint the Empire is pro market so guess what I did…). Again, the vast majority of video games and movies, even those which do contain violence, have an ultimate good versus an ultimate evil. I do not believe that entertainment is actually encouraging unjustified, random violence. It's just simply not, therefore this issue is a distraction from more important things.

We need to also reiterate the fact that the Department of Justice reports violent crimes, in general, are in decline.-1. I couldn't find anything newer at the time of this writing, but if you have a newer one please get it to me. So far, I have yet to read any press release indicating an uptick in violent crimes since 2009. The reality is violent crimes are in decline. Pretending otherwise is just disingenuousness and denial on the part of the talking heads. Ergo, there is no need to be calling for censorship. Besides, why would we want to do with government what the market gives us tools to deal with on our own?

Consider this: When *Atlas Shrugged* finally got a film adaptation, did we go see it? Did we buy it? What message does that send Hollywood? What do you think our inaction sent to Hollywood? What does it tell them when we go see super violent movies like *Kill Bill*, but aren't there for more conservative films like *Atlas Shrugged*?

Recently there have been a lot of conservative pundits the Conservative leaning Bat-Man movies. The shooting in Colorado, which occurred at a screening of the latest Batman, involved a shooter who was mentally ill and identified with the villain, the Joker. The Joker was not portrayed as being in any way heroic. Batman was the hero because he stopped the Joker's killing spree. It's classic good versus evil, there's no conditioning kids to be killers here. The film was a comment about the need to stop terrorists at all costs, something we on the Right tend to agree with. The Third Batman was a blatant swipe at Occupy Wall Street, warning viewers of the dangers of class warfare. Somehow the positives got buried under the fact that one guy, who happened to be a paranoid schizophrenic, identified with the Joker, who was portrayed as being a psychopath in the first place. The Batman Trilogy is filled with great Conservative values, we ought to embrace these films! Instead, some are coming just shy of calling for the films to be banned.

Most movies do not glorify violence. Most movies, left or right, are simply good standing up to evil, that is why we cheer; not because we have conditioned to believe that every time someone dies on screen we get a piece of popcorn, as Colonel Grossman alleged on the 1-13-13 episode of Beck's show, comparing human beings to Pavlov's dog. To me, this is seriously dehumanizing and intolerant. It pre-supposes that men are nothing more than animals and ignores the fact that for every study linking violence to media, there's one that shows there is no such link. Seriously, do a google search, the amount of contradictory studies out there is staggering. Since the time I wrote this Glenn Beck, a man I normally see eye to eye with, authored a new book called *Control,* which features a section on video games that needs a specific and detailed response. It will necessitate a chapter all its own much later in this book as we take it to press. This chapter is more a response to the endless calls for censorship, whereas that chapter is a response specifically to Beck's book.

Glenn Beck is usually an independent thinker, which is why both Republicans and Democrats hate him while independents love him. However, on this issue, I believe he is wrong. I also am saddened by the fact that he is willing to examine the facts and defend one's right to bear arms, but when there are facts that disprove his thesis about media violence causing violence, he doesn't seem aware of, or even willing to look for an antithetical argument to make sure he's right. Normally he does, and to his credit he leads with corrections when in error, which is why I like and respect him. Still, on this one issue, he is just wrong. He mocks those who say "I've played those games, I turned out fine," but that is the ultimate test. Of the millions of people who watched Batman how many shot up a movie theatre claiming to be the villain? One. Of the millions of people who played Call of Duty and games like it, how many have gone and shot up their class mates? Almost none, maybe one if it is true that Adam Lanza was playing it, but CBS pulled the article claiming that. I will argue that it is valid to say, I play those kinds of games. I just like saving innocent people from a malevolent evil. We are drawn to this entertainment because we like to root for the heroes and we like to be the hero. We like to see evil defeated. I turned out just fine, thank you. Well, a bit pudgy but otherwise fine.

Gangs violence and mass murder all predate the existence of video games. What games influenced Jimmy Hoffa? What games influenced Adolf Hitler or Stalin, or Mao, or Pol Pott or Che Guevara? These were sick mad who would have done what they did, whether video games and movies existed or not. Before these mediums existed, people of the Right blamed Rock and Roll, before that jazz. I can't remember who said it but one rocker, in response to his critics said, and I agree, that if you go around killing people because some f--- with a guitar tells you to then you're pretty messed up anyway and would do it with or without that musician's influence.

Like it or not the first amendment guarantees *everyone* and even teams of people (aka corporations), the right to express themselves how they see fit. Whether or not to censor the media is the wrong argument considering that all of these shooters end up literally being mentally ill. Even if it was the right argument , these things exist because YOU buy them. Where were you for Atlas Shrugged? Part one was a decent movie, yet it bombed ensuring part two had a worse cast, and an even smaller budget. You weren't there for that one either, so if there is a part three at all it's probably going to fare even worse! Where were you for The Voyage of the Dawn Treader? A wholesome Christ centered film. If you want more wholesome entertainment tell Hollywood and the game industry by literally putting your money where your mouth is, or shut up. I was there for Atlas Shrugged part one and two. I was there for Voyage of the Dawn Treader. I wrote and promoted blogs for all of them encouraging people to get out the door and support these films. I even took people to see them at my own expense, because I knew they were in danger of bombing despite being decent films. If you aren't actively using the market to try and steer the ship of culture then you have no right to complain. Hollywood and video games are a reflection of the culture, not the other way around. They know where the culture is because they keep track of what the culture is buying. They have to. They have to know where the money is.

It would surprise many that this Jeffersonian-Republican and political activist didn't used to care about politics at all. The first election I was old enough to participate in was the now infamous Bush v Gore. I was actually going to vote for Gore because I do not believe in dynasties, but then he scared me off when he promised to give the entertainment industry six months to clean up their act should he be elected... or else.

Worse he brought on anti-gaming activist Joe Liberman as his running mate. You know, the guy that continued to push for government censorship, even after the market created the ESRB to self-regulate violent video games. The guy who called on the government to act, even after his former side-kick on the right, John McCain, announced the free-market based ESRB was an adequate solution... ? That guy! AKA Senator Palpatine...

At any rate, Gore's vow to take on the video game industry was a small, barely noticed blip on the radar issue for most. Likely most of you won't even remember it, but for me it was a huge issue. Why? Well Mormon I may be but I grew up in an era of mass desensitization and confess to not being as easily offended as my elders. I grew up on Mortal Kombat, Doom, Wolfenstein, etc. I grew up with the Matrix, Terminator, Jaws and Jurassic Park. However I came out okay. Again, Glenn Beck is now mocking people like me, yet we are the 99% of people who play video games and watch violent movies. I don't exactly have an extensive criminal record ya know, in fact many of my friends are police, lawyers and legislators. I love and respect them all even when we disagree on some issues as I am sure some may here.

I once attended a Young Republicans presentation by Utah's controversial Eagle Forum. Now, I love these guys half the time and I civilly disagree with them the other half. In example, I think their stance on the Con Con (which we will explore in a later project) is a lot of fear mongering which is preventing a civil and rational discussion that I think this nation *needs* to have... if only as an absolute last resort. Nevertheless, I agree with them on Common Core, States Rights and a number of other key issues. However, I had a hard time holding my tongue when the speaker started berating video games and the former Utah State Attorney General Mark Shurtleff, who stood up for the free market and fought against legislation designed to criminalize selling certain games to minors (an event which almost never happens as selling T and M rated games to underage players is both against every store's policy.) -1) Sales of games to minors at all is also impractical, as kids almost never have the $60.00 cash needed, since their parents command the almighty wallet. Games are a mightily expensive hobby and the idea that a six year old would wander into Gamestop alone with $60 worth of cash is laughable.

Mark Shurtleff's position on this matter was dead on correct. Monitoring what games kids are playing is the job of the parents, not the state, period. Irony is that, as I recall, Eagle Forum has pushed for parents to take over Sex Ed and getting it out of the public schools, a position I happen to agree with, but if it's the parent's job to teach kids about sex, it's their job to stay on top of what games their kids are playing... or are they even playing?

The market is changing, and in fact Sony, Microsoft and Nintendo all lost huge amounts of money in 2012. A lot of experts credit that to the advent of the smart phone and the I-Pad. Kids are just not playing games the way their parents are, in fact a new study shows that the average gamer is now over 30 (-2) , which makes sense because I am 33 and my wife is approaching her 30s as well. We have not been blessed with children, but we do have nieces and god children who we do not allow to be exposed to mature games. We take that responsibility very seriously. Kids within our sphere of influence get Mario and Sonic. The adults get that plus whatever game features a planet that needs saving but features a little more violence than kicking turtles. While there is one of those kids, approaching his late teens, still plays on the consoles, most of the younger kids are more interested in the innocent Angry Birds than they are Mario and Yoshi, let alone Mortal Kombat. Try separating my 8 year old niece from here generic Ipad... Ain't gonna happen... But even when they do play on the consoles, they are skipping through the story sequences and getting right to the action sequences, unlike me, I watch every story sequence with zeal... They just don't have the attention span for the stories and they don't play on the consoles long either. They only play until they quickly get bored, then it's back to the tablet. They want to hop on, play for a few minutes and then go do something else.

Tastes between the generations are not the same. Attention spans are not the same. The market for the very games that Glenn Beck and the Eagle Forum are concerned about has aged. The kids grew up and became parents, not criminals. Their kids aren't interested in the same kinds of entertainment in the I-pad era, rendering the whole debate over criminalizing game sales moot.

But even if it wasn't moot... look I don't like some of the content which ends up in some of the games out there, but I cannot use the government as a tool to impose my beliefs on the masses. It is hypocritical for me to expect Liberals to stay out of my wallet if they cannot expect me to stay out of their private lives. Simply put, the Free Market must sort this out. There's a reason there's several new Mario games each year, while Mortal Kombat only rears its ugly head once in a blue moon. Most games sold are neither to minors nor are they M rated. A better approach for those concerned about violence in media, is to take the initiative to buy their kids and grandkids the more child friendly games for Christmas. To Beck's credit, he has made clear he is already taking this approach. However, odds are that if it isn't a quick, easy game on a cell phone it won't get played. This goes back to my original point that this argument is moot since kids are neither buying nor playing the games in question. Those that are tend to be either approaching, or are already, 30 and raising families, not committing violent crime.

The compromise on the issue of media is simple. You don't have to buy it, but you shouldn't have the power to stop me from doing it, or any other law abiding citizen. To say, as alleged by Colonel Grossman, that our motive for playing violent video games is because we are being conditioned to take pleasure from killing is disgusting, insulting, dehumanizing and brutally dishonest. The fact is we play the games and watch the movies we do because we all long to be or root for the hero. We all want to save the world, drive the BMW, get the latest Q Branch gadget and win the heart of the girl. We fall in love with the characters and the story, which almost always involves a great good overcoming a great evil. It's really quite that simple. We all want to experience the Hero's Journey. Movies, and video games in particular, allow us that fantasy, even if only for a few hours.

Moreover it's worth pointing out that in the most recent massacres none of the perpetrators have been under the age of eighteen. In other words, you can't use these events as evidence that kids are being turned into monsters by movies or video games when kids aren't the perpetrators. They're adults.

See, I told you no one was safe! Now I like Glenn Beck and the Eagle Forum quite a bit. Although the left wing media has a different perspective, I believe both are a force for good, though I fear both will hate my guts and see me damned to Hell (Michigan) for this book. I am a Blaze subscriber and a proud fellow Skousenite (fan of Cleon Skousen), but the odds are they won't like me after reading this.

I did warn that I was prepared to skewer everyone, so now let me skewer the left, because again, the common thread in these shootings isn't the guns either. It's the fact that they're all mentally ill, and it's you lefties fault they are on the streets and not in an institution, where they can do no harm. If I were to propose institutionalizing the deeply disturbed and mentally ill, we both know you would object. All the movies you've made about the horrors of institutions tell me so (most recently the highly underrated and artistically brilliant Sucker Punched.) Still, as awesome and terrifying as these movies are, you have poisoned the public against these institutions which could help these people. If nothing else. they would at least keep these disturbed individuals off the street.

The left loves to start interviews this way, the setup is to ask someone right leaning if they agree with a quote and then... well I'm getting ahead of myself. Let me ask you folks on the left, do you agree with the following:

> This year will go down in history. Fort the first time, a civilized nation has full gun registration. Our streets will be safer, our police more efficient, and the world will follow our lead into the future!

Ready? You just agreed with *Adolf Hitler*! Now here's the trick, Hitler went on to ban guns for non-Germans. How did that work out for the Jews who were denied the right to keep and bear their arms? And here's what's even funnier, this position on gun control is actually less extreme than the position taken by the modern left. I'm not going to scream "Nazi, Nazi, Nazi," because that's what you do, but I am going to put forward that gun control only hurts the law abiding citizen. Look, murder was already illegal and it didn't stop the Sandy Hook shooter from killing 26 people. Just because a law is in place doesn't mean that a criminal or mentally ill person is going to abide by it. Look, liberty is messy, but it requires that the majority of people not be punished for the mistakes or crimes of the few.

If you are going to pretend you care about the ninety-nine percent than you have to recognize a single mathematical fact. Millions of Americans are gun owners and less than 1% of those go on shooting sprees, moreover, it is no coincidence that these shootings occur largely in "gun free" zones where people are unable to defend themselves. Crap like this doesn't happen in Utah, because when it does the shooter is stopped.

A few years ago there was an incident at our Trolley Square Mall, but the shooter didn't get far before he was put down by a concealed carry permit holder, who also happened to be an off duty police officer. Other stories we get here in Utah go as follows: a burglar breaks into a house and takes the home owner hostage, the home owner tells the burglar he needs to get the key to his safe and withdraws a fire arm from his coat, then takes the burglar down. Another example is in West Valley, where a burglar was climbing through a window and the home owner shot him dead as he was half way in. When an emergency happens and seconds matter, the fire arm is handy, the police are minutes away. It's not like you can have a police station in the basement of every home. It takes time for them to arrive, and while you wait, you and your family could end up dead, or worse. That is why the right to bear arms should not be interfered with.

On the rare occasion where there is a violent crime in Utah it often ends badly for the criminal. We don't actually have the kind of crime you see in Chicago or

New York here. The reason for the difference in crime rates is that we pretty much all carry firearms, and criminals know that breaking into any house in Utah is a potentially fatal error. That is a good thing because it keeps crime at bay. For myself, I myself have eight different means of dispatching an intruder and that is not counting the many more swords I have. Breaking into my house is an extremely dangerous endeavor and that is how it ought to be. We should all have this kind of security.

In my own experience, I lived in an apartment complex where there were regular attempts to break in, we had a 52 inch TV you see… so I got my Rugar P-89, which I call Jefferson. We were very open with our neighbors that my wife and I bore arms now. Suddenly the break in attempts stopped. Incidentally, when we moved to Tooele we had to leave the TV behind with a neighbor, the one who lived immediately to the left of our apartment. She is a left leaner and didn't believe in guns, so naturally one can guess what happened to the TV. Yup, it got stolen. It's okay though, I bought a bigger TV to replace it and it does full Stereo 3D which helps Assassins Creed 3 look amazing! But don't even think about it… if you don't fear the idea of me with an arsenal, remember always, my wife grew up in Texas.

In Utah, we don't hear about violent crime a lot, but when we do there's ample heroics of ordinary citizens which often puts an abrupt end to what could have been a horrible situation otherwise. More important is that, while there were many issues where the Founding Fathers did not agree with each other, the use and possession of fire arms was not one of those issues. There was, in fact, near universal agreement amongst them. The Second Amendment wasn't just about forming a militia, it was ensuring that the people had the right to bear arms as well. It's all about how they would define militia. George Mason put it best saying, "I ask, Sir, what is the militia? It is the whole people. To disarm the people is the best and most effectual way to enslave them."-3. This attitude was ubiquitous. You see to most of them we, all of us are the militia. Richard Henry Lee would write "A militia, when properly formed, are in fact the people themselves..."-4

Now that this is out of the way, let's get into the nuts and bolts as to why. It's because the Founders, both Federalist and Republican, had no love of leviathan government and both parties feared that if the people were stripped of their guns they would be subjected to the same horrors of tyranny that they had fought against. Nowhere does it say the Second Amendment is for hunting. It's about the right of the people to defend themselves against the government, and with government growing to a tyrannical level of control under both Bush and Obama, one can see the Founders had good cause to fear. James Madison wrote, "The highest number to which, according to the best computation, a standing army can be carried in any country, does not exceed one hundredth part of the whole number of souls; or one twenty-fifth part of the number able to bear arms. This proportion would not yield, in the United States, an army of more than twenty-five or thirty thousand men. To these would be opposed a militia amounting to near half a million of citizens with arms in their hands, officered by men chosen from among themselves, fighting for the common liberties and united and conducted by governments possessing their affections and confidence. It may well be doubted whether a militia thus circumstanced could ever be conquered by such a proportion of regular troops. Those who are best acquainted with the late successful resistance of this country against the British arms will be most inclined to deny the possibility of it. Besides the advantage of being armed, which the Americans possess over the people of almost every other nation, the existence of subordinate governments, to which the people are attached and by which the militia officers are appointed, forms a barrier against the enterprises of ambition, more insurmountable than any which a simple government of any form can admit of. Notwithstanding the military establishments of the several kingdoms of Europe, which are carried as far as the public resources will bear, *the governments are afraid to trust the people with arms.*"(Federalist Papers 46, 1788) Patrick Henry would say, "Guard with jealous attention the public liberty. Suspect everyone who approaches that jewel. Unfortunately, nothing will preserve it but downright force. Whenever you give up that force, you are inevitably ruined."-5

Thomas Pane, the leftist of the group, would write, "Arms like laws discourage and keep the invader and the plunderer in awe, and preserve order in the world as well as property. The balance of power is the scale of peace. The same balance would be preserved were the entire world destitute of arms, for all would be alike; *but since some will not others dare not lay them aside.* And while a single nation refuses to lay them down, it is proper that all should keep them up. Horrid mischief would ensue were one half the world deprived of the use of them; for while avarice and ambition have a place in the heart of man, the weak will become a prey to the strong. The history of every age and nation establishes these truths, and facts need but little arguments when they prove themselves." -6

Thomas Jefferson wrote, "No freeman shall be debarred the use of arms within his own lands."-7

But why should I waste time trying to argue the values of the Founders with you? You Liberals respond to this sort of stuff one of three ways 1) Dismiss it, "you're just getting that from Beck." Nope, "well then you're just getting that from Skousen!" Whatever, I usually prefer to read the books written in the time the event happened. Everything written after that is subject to spin, so on to your next action. What is ironic about the Liberal first response is that, in my experience, it is exactly what they do do themselves. They fall back to what is being taught by their liberal professors, or something they can look up in an internet chat room briefly, or Wikipedia. It is seldom I have someone who can put together a counter-quote or resource proving me wrong, instead they just deny my source's legitimacy, then lead the conversation down to an unfruitful, "na-ah," "uh-huh," which makes discussing history and philosophy a fruitless venture. 2) Building from step one; Deny the legitimacy of the quote itself. "George Washington wouldn't have said that," whatever. 3) Blast its relevance in the modern world. By now if you're a liberal reading this you've done all three. I've spent years studying these men. I feel like I know them well, but I've also spent years debating with liberals. Anything which proves liberals wrong is inevitably ignored in some fashion or another, even to the point that Paul Krugman declared that "Conservative facts are non-facts," which is sad because, in addition to that statement being complete nonsense, it puts up a shield that makes real discussion impossible. Without being able to get through to you liberals, we have no way of helping you to realize just how tyrannical your party really is. Also Krugman suggested that faking a space alien invasion would save the economy, so there you go. Don't feel bad though, my party is a bunch of pansies... I also won't bother arguing statistics, besides they coincide with what I wrote about video games anyway, an irony missed by the authors of "Control." It's hard to argue that violent crime is on the decline with a party who ignores statistics and convinces themselves that things are worse than ever.

There is simple point to be made on this matter, Salt Lake City is pretty safe and Utah has very relaxed gun laws. Chicago is very dangerous, in contrast, and Illinois, especially Chicago itself, has very strict gun laws. Connecticut already has an AR Weapons ban for its state and the Clinton AR Weapons ban was already in effect when Columbine happened. Mass murders still occurred with those respective bans in place. Here in Utah, many teachers are Concealed Carry Permit holders and *do* conceal, and *do* carry. Still, the tendency for violent crimes that we have seen in Ney York and Chicago never seem to happen here. Based on that (granted anecdotal) evidence, our way seems to work better, but facts be damned.

Cars kill more people every year than guns, but considering that the DNC is dominated by enviro-nuts I don't think it's going to take long before Diane Feinstein proposes a nutty car ban...

Whether you contest the disputed Washington declaration of fire arms as Liberty's teeth or not it is true. You cannot have a free people if those people are unarmed, but as it stands, I am already convinced that Liberals are all hell bent on what some would describe as a monarchy anyway... What the heck, Obama is a monarchist... The monarch, of course, isn't going to want his subjects armed. Do you think the surf or peasant farmer was allowed to have swords? We ought to celebrate the fact that America has so many gun owners. The fact that the ninety-nine percent of them have not been involved in any violent crime is, in and of itself, a marvel.

On a personal note, I have what Liberals would call an Assault Rifle, what is properly called ArmaLite after the company which originally designed the guns in question. I bought it as a joke. It scared everyone in my house, except my wife, until they learned two facts, 1st, it's only a .22 (a needle thrower, as those bullets are so small they couldn't even penetrate a pumpkin we brought to the local range) and 2nd, it was not what my brother called a "spray and pray." These weapons are not automatic weapons. There are, therefore, not military grade. Although I believe I should be able to get those weapons, they are not available in the open market without expensive licensing and permitting. Also, Full-Auto weapons are cost prohibitive. Functionally, my Mosberg .22 AR rifle is no different than my wife's Marlin .22 hunting rifle. Why do I have it then? Because I like to set up soda cans in the middle of the canyons, against a backdrop and shoot them. It's a bit of a hick sport, but it is a sport nonetheless. And now to take a puck shot at myself. I also serve as living proof that video games and marksmanship are not interchangeable. I am a very good shot with a rifle in real life, however I suck with a shotgun and am even worse with a hand gun. Worse yet I am always the first to go down in multi-player Halo.

The compromise on this is simple. The American people were intended from the beginning to be armed. States with fewer gun restrictions tend to have fewer incidents of gun violence than states with stricter gun laws. "Gun free zones" tend to be an open invitation to crazy people. That does not mean we can't do anything. The left and the right promoting bans on anything are both wrong. The inanimate objects are not the culprit. Bans will only affect law abiding citizen negatively, as the criminal mind does not exactly abide by the law. Rather, we should be looking at the common thread no one is talking about which is mental health.

The recent incidents of violence almost all feature a mentally ill patient with people around him who knew he was dangerous. In the case of the Colorado Batman shootings, the perpetrator had been seeing a shrink who was in possession of his writings which should have given cause for concern. The shrink failed to act on it. The shooter responsible for maiming Gabby Giffords had plenty of material he posted to the web which was incoherent, nutty and threatening. No one decided to keep an eye on him. Finally, the perpetrator at Sandy Hook also killed his mother, who was reaching out for help in such a way which lead him to believe she was going to send him away. Sadly, he probably should have been put away a long time ago.

At least in the Sandy Hook incident the perpetrator did not own the guns that were used, they were his mother's. No one sold him those weapons. I will admit I don't know how the guns in the other recent incidents were acquired, but I don't think there would be many who would disagree with requiring a deeper background check, so long as it is a state background check and not a federal one. This could help identify paranoid schizophrenics and then deny them the sale of a firearm. Doing this won't stop mentally ill and dangerous people from getting firearms, but it will certainly help people feel like we've done something, which is what I think the public wants. This would be the least invasive solution. It would stop direct sales of these tools to dangerously mentally ill people, which, I imagine, isn't something that happens often anyway. Still, it's a good step to take, so long as it is possible to get yourself off any "mentally ill" lists the government makes, once you can show adequate evidence of a full recovery.

More than that, though, we need to look at how we're approaching mental illness. People who were so mentally ill that they could not function in a normal society should not be out on the street. These folks show up a lot around the public transports in Salt Lake City. They're pretty scary and when I have to use public transportation, I sometimes wish I didn't always leave Jefferson at home. I take comfort in knowing that most folks around me likely do have a fire arm, should anything happen and I can just hide behind them. These people don't just talk to themselves, they argue with themselves, often in a very loud and disruptive manner. They threaten passersbys and when they ride the train with you they smell like burnt ham sprinkled with 3 day old uncooked fish... You think me heartless, but the thought of someone like this owning a gun is scary to me because I doubt that mutually assured destruction would be much of a deterrent to them. It is, however, enough to keep the sane criminal at bay.

This is the problem I feel we need to solve, especially since mental illness always has a role to play whenever a mass shooting occurs. It is unfortunate that it is only briefly touched upon by the media, before the right starts blaming video games no one plays and the left blames guns in general. If you're looking to solve a problem, you need to look at policies that will actually solve the problem. Guns have been around for about 300 years, yet school shootings like this seem to be a more recent (though very rare) issue, so guns aren't the problem. These school shootings seem to have started in the late seventies when the only video game on the market was Pong... And as previously mentioned, real life violence has been in decline in more recent years as the games have grown more realistic and more... and then less violent. Though many games still contain the killing of human beings, it is not bereft of a moral cause (saving the world from a great evil, IE Nazis, Commies or those awful dragons that are always mucking things up.) It seems unproductive to ignore the facts and to seek solutions which would infringe upon people's liberty when a more conventional answer is there, buried under the rhetoric.

Wasn't it around the seventies where we saw a move away from institutionalizing the mentally ill? Is it coincidence that all of these mass murderers seem to be dangerously mentally ill? Could it be that the real reason this is happening isn't because of guns and games but because we are no longer willing to take the issue of mental illness seriously? Just a thought.

Chapter 2 references:

-1Key Facts at a glance-Bureau of Justice Statistics http://bjs.ojp.usdoj.gov/content/glance/tables/viortrdtab.cfm Retrieved 1-3-13

-2 http://e3.gamespot.com/story/6380546/average-age-of-us-gamers-now-30

-3 George Mason, co Author of the Second Amendment during the Virginia Convention to Ratify the Constitution, 1788

-4 *Richard Henry Lee* writing in *Letters from the Federal Farmer to the Republic*, Letter XVIII, May, 1788.

-5 Virginia's U.S. Constitution ratification convention (June 5, 1788), reported in Elliot, *Debates of the Several State Conventions* 3:45.

-6 Thomas Paine, Thoughts On Defensive War, 1775.

-7 Proposed Virginia Constitution. Compiled by Paul Leicester Ford The writings of Thomas Jefferson Vol. 2:27 (1776)

Chapter 3: The Income Crap

The Bible says, "for ye have the poor always with you..." (Mat. 26:11 KJV). That's not to say that helping the poor is not a noble venture, but nowhere in the Bible is turning over all our stuff to the government endorsed as the means of eliminating poverty. If it was, then the Bible has been utterly discredited. We have been waging a war on poverty for some time now, and it is not by government that things have improved but by innovations of the "evil" 1%. Where would you be without Bill Gates building Windows in his garage some thirty years ago? Where would you be without Steve Jobs pushing the IPhone to market? Heck where would I be without Nintendo? I'd have gone crazy a long time ago!

I am grateful for our entrepreneurs. Even though I am poor, (though if this book sells a few million copies I won't be. So go buy a copy for your friends!) I live in relative comfort. It is not government programs that allow me to be comfortable while living in some 400 square feet. It is the fact that free market innovations have brought me a super-powerful mega-computer in a small box, a thin and flat 3D monitor, a decent sized flat 3D TV, across from it a decent bed, just about every game console known to man, a 1,000 plus movie collection and some 400 plus video games. Now, those collections have been being built since I was a kid so don't harp on me. I am also very frugal, so believe it or not, I didn't spend all that much on these things, I'm very good at taking advantage of clearance sales.

I used to have massive debt though, and it caused my own financial collapse. But unlike congress, I have been laser focused on eliminating my debt. You can help by buying this book! Buy two! Anyway, the result of my wife's and my previous recklessness with money is that we are renting out a tiny basement, which is very dusty and hard to keep clean. I am on the verge of being laid off from the highest paying job I have ever had and likely will have lost it by the time you read this. In spite of my life's shortcomings, I know one fact to be true, I have a lot of nice creature comforts compared to kids in Africa. In fact, comparatively, I have no clue what poverty is and frankly neither do you.

Politicians have been promoting class warfare as an excuse to grow government. Part of that has been this massive media push on the growing income gap as the world's most pressing issue. It's not the fault of some rich guy in New York that I spent myself into Oblivion (a very fun video game by the way), nor is it the fault of the guy who invented Facebook. I have no cause to blame my employer for my problems, whoever that will be by the time this work is published. In fact, I am grateful to my employer for giving me a means by which I can earn a living with dignity and honor.

Now, there are jobs I won't take because the pay and work environment are too poor, but the beauty of a free market is that I get to sell my services to an employer and I get to set a price for my work. Alternatively, they can make an offer and then I can decide for myself if that is enough. It is then my choice what to do with my money. It is not the rich guy threatening me with jail if I refuse their services, that would be the IRS.

Right off the bat, when I get my check, before the bank even gets the money several hundred dollars are taken from me without me having a say in it at all. Some Republicans say that poor folks like myself get more back than we pay in... Well now we know why you lost the election, because for me that is simply not true. No, instead I usually have to pay in at the end of the year, even though I claim only 1 and have the government take an extra 10% just trying to avoid having to pay in, but alas no. I get soaked.. By the way, my wife claims 0, and also has an extra 10% taken to try and prevent this and it's not working.

Making this even worse is the fact that if I get a raise, or if I get promoted, the government takes that much more making my pay increases imperceptible. My Dad makes twice what I do, yet our checks are comparable because of taxes. The more the government takes, the less you can save, the less you can save the less wealth you can accumulate, the less you can accumulate the less wealthy you can become, hence the wealth gap.

All the taxes we have, (federal, state, local, plus all the penalties, corporate, capital gains taxes, etc.) strip the wealthy of their superfluous earnings, leaving them less to pay you. That is unfortunately why I lost the best job I ever had. The state of the economy is not good and our client decided the service we provided was superfluous, so our project was ended because our client now has to pay more in taxes at a time when business has slowed, so naturally they had to make budget cuts.

The reason I bring this up is because the tradeoff for the soak the rich crap is that the rich have less money, but if you think that will close the income gap, you're fool headed. Rather than closing the income gap these policies will cause the income gap to widen, as the rich will take fewer risks on you and will want your services cheaper. Hence, a job that would have paid $12.00 an hour eight years ago now only pays $9.00. This isn't economic theory it's economic fact. You do it too.

When you are having financial difficulties do you continue to pay that $75.00 a month for Direct TV? Nope, you reduce your package to the minimalist $50 package and when your budget continues to tighten you eventually drop it all together, or buy a Roku. It's this very phenomenon that is wreaking havoc on the video game industry. Since the economy collapsed in 2007 (after the Democrats won the House and Senate in massive numbers by the way, and Bush refused to veto any of their bills) people have lost their jobs, when they have found new jobs the pay has been less than what they were previously accustom to. As a result many former gamers had no choice but to get rid of the extras, so game sales dropped dramatically, since then the following companies have all closed their doors due to slowed sales:

Radical		Entertainment			2012
38	Studios		-		2012
Big	Huge	Games		-	2012
THQ	San	Diego		-	2012
Zipper	Interactive		-		2012
Gusto	Games		-		2012

4mm	Games		-	2012
Eden	Games		-	2012
dtp	Entertainment		-	2012
Black	Hole	Entertainment	-	2012
Spellbound	Entertainment		-	2012
Artech	Studios		-	2011
Dark	Energy	Digital	-	2012
Hudson	Soft		-	2012
Reakktor	Media		-	2012
Ubisoft			Vancouver	
-		2012		

Furthermore Square-Enix, Konami, Capcom, Sony, Nintendo and Microsoft have all been facing stormy waters, as all of them have had weaker sales in recent years than what has been hoped for. People just don't have the extra money. You make cuts to your budget to try and preserve what wealth you have, why would you expect the rich to behave any differently from you?

That is the biggest problem with class warfare, it dehumanizes a political target and tries to make this group or that "the other." I have a number of very wealthy friends. One of them is so generous that he won't let any of his guests pay for their own drinks or meals. I have a hard time with the *rich are monsters* narrative that is being sold to us, ironically, by the even more rich. People like George Soros. Soros is a chief financier of Occupy Wall Street through his Open Society Institute. OSI channeled his money to Ad Busters, the chief organizers of the fake movement. He has spent billions trying to gin up a false narrative that, somehow, the fact that you are poor is a direct result of the fact that someone else is rich. I'm highly suspicious of Soros and others like him, including Warren Buffett, because I can't see how attacking a system that benefitted them so well makes any sense unless you're a twisted outside the box thinker (which I happen to be.)

Let's put on our smiley-faced, tinfoil hat for a second here, because I will own up and admit that the following is conjecture. I have no proof, but strongly suspect this is what is happening. If you are an opportunist, (which in my mind is different than a capitalist) you know the primary threat to your wealth is competition. If you are an opportunist who has already made your fortune, then you are in a unique position to stifle your competition by promoting taxes that won't touch what you have in the bank already, but will stop an up and comer from having the funds necessary to challenge you in an open market. So if you're Warren Buffett, what's your incentive to tell the public the truth about your pay? That you collect it in capital gains to avoid the now 40% income tax. Why not just lie and tell people your secretary has a higher tax rate than you? You already have $33 Billion dollars banked, you have your reward. Now the fun is in keeping that money in the bank, and the only way to do that is not to spend it. The best way to do that is to avoid investing in your own business on ways to improve, because your competition is doing something better than you. Why bother with all that nasty competition when you can just get their taxes raised to crush the competition without you having to lift a finger?

Let's face it, if the super-rich are truly evil as Occupy suggests, would it be beyond reason to assume that the super-rich may have selfish motives for backing tyrannical tax proposals? This is why I do not trust the super-rich or their mega-corporations. The capitalist, in contrast to the opportunist, embraces competition as a challenge to improve. In another amusing anecdote, Warren Buffett is currently fighting with the IRS over one billion dollars, so much for wanting to pay his fair share.

Okay, tin foil hat is off now. In some strange way, the idea of opportunistic billionaires manipulating the public to crush their would be competitors through tax policies makes a lot more sense than billionaires waging war on themselves. I don't believe Soros or Buffett are rigid ideologues. I don't think they believe the crap that comes out of their mouths. All I know is that when I get a pay raise, it's hardly noticeable after the government gets done with it. That certainly stops me from being able to compete with the likes of Buffett and Soros, unless this book sells 33 billion copies. Even if that does happen, after the feds take their 40 percent and the state, payroll, sales and property taxes are done with me then I will be left with only about 40% of that 33 billion which means, thanks to the Progressive tax policies, I CAN'T get as rich as those that already are and THAT is not fair. THAT is why there's such a huge income gap; because the laws are being written to put a cap on YOU. Don't think for a second the Democrats (or Republicans for that matter) would ever pass a tax policy that would cut into their chief financiers. Hell, Soros practically owns the Democratic party. In some cases, he owns them quite literally, e.g. some of their propaganda arms like Media Matters and Moveon.org.

More importantly, there is a freedom issue at hand. The British love to complain that the Revolutionary War (really the first of many anti-colonialist battles Britain had to fight and would lose) was unnecessary because the taxes that were being asked of them were miniscule. Comparatively speaking, this is a truism. The Revolutionary war began as an anti-tax revolt. For some, the anger was in that they had no representation in parliament, but for others, it was the effect of taxes on liberty.

Taxes are a necessary evil, but it doesn't take much for them to become tyrannical. Taxes should be small enough to be relatively unnoticeable. Government should be small enough to be relatively unnoticeable. When the Founders began their new American adventure, there was only a relatively modest tariff on imported goods. Jefferson was fine with this consumption driven tax because it was a tax mostly paid by the rich who could afford to pay. It was a tax that the poor were also able to avoid. This modest revenue source managed to pay the cost of government just fine, and incredibly, they managed to pay off the national debt shortly after the election of the first Democrat Andrew Jackson. Jackson would then, of course, move on to using tax payer dollars to reward his supporters (kind of like how Democrats pass emergency stimulus bills which transfers tax payer dollars to the Labor Unions)... and so began the spoils system which exists to this day. Today, however, the government has grown to enormous levels. Between the wars we fight and our unsustainable welfare system, we are constantly broke. Democrats won't cut a dime to save their lives but, it needs to happen.

The American Spoils system is supposed to be gone now, but it's not. There's all kinds of special interest groups that benefit from both sides of the isle. Have you ever noticed that GE has gotten away with paying no taxes ever since Obama became President? How about Solyndra? $500 million tax payer dollars shipped their way, only for them to take that money, close their doors and walk away with fatter pockets. Someone should have gone to jail for that. Think about it. They got a $500 million dollar wealth transfer and respond by closing their doors and laying off all their workers. So much for Democrats supporting the labor movement.

Republicans engage in this crap too, so don't let them get off the hook, Halliburton anyone? I don't oppose corporations and unions getting involved with politics, but common values and ideas should be the basis for supporting a candidate. Instead, corporations and unions use their money and influence to buy favors in the form of wealth redistribution. They take income from the tax payers like you and I and give it to the corporate fat cats on Wall Street. Meanwhile, Main Street is having a harder time putting food on the table.

The government tells you now that we can't do a nominal fair tax instead of our income tax because the responsibilities of the government are too great. Is it the government's responsibility to spend millions and billions to study pig odor, to build robot squirrels, to study "Mormon" crickets? This is why Bob Bennett was booted by the way. Only a super-rich dude would fancy such luxuries as necessary and proper. That is what happens when you are so far removed from the responsibilities of running a business, making pay roll or punching in at 9am and out at 5pm (let alone the night shift).

There is all kinds of frivolities being funded by the government, and it has been written about and discussed by numerous writers far more popular and talented than I. I'm just a guy who has to punch in at 9am and out at 5pm and fears the impact of a night shift on my health and my family. I'm also a nerd who is fascinated by history and economics. Besides, this book will become very long if I start listing off all the ways the government wastes your money, instead I will appeal to your memory. Remember how you felt about these things in 2010? Do you remember why? Why did the Tea Party appear on the scene? 1 Trillion dollars in last minute spending by Bush, followed by Obama opening up his term with another 1 trillion dollars in additional spending, a half trillion dollar omnibus spending bill, then another two trillion dollar health care bill... Boom... Taxpayer Hulk-out!

Obviously, that movement came and went (please someone prove me wrong), but there were reasons it emerged. The sad reality is though; it failed to do anything significant to stop the spending. Obama and the Democrat's crushing defeat in 2010 only caused them to double down and the GOP was just not willing enough to fight it out to lead... and so since Obama did lead and John Boehner didn't Obama was re-elected and immediately raised taxes.

The simple fact is there's a few trillion, of that sixteen trillion in debt, that could be cut. A lot of it is just waste and luxury pet projects. We could make those cuts well before we would need to even talk about entitlements. Now on entitlements, even FA Hayek agreed that a marginal safety net was necessary, but I am not so sure. I think there is a good argument to be made that taking the fruits of labor from the laborer, by means of force, to ensure the safety of another, is immoral. However, charity is the highest morality, aside from liberty, to which we may aspire, but charity is voluntary and taxes are not.

Jefferson said, "To take from one because it is thought that his own industry and that of his father's has acquired too much, in order to spare others who, or whose fathers, have not exercised equal industry and skill, is to violate arbitrarily the first principal of association, 'the guarantee to everyone a free exercise of his industry, and the fruits acquired by it.' If the overgrown wealth of an individual be deemed dangerous to the state, the best corrective law of equal inheritance to all his descendants in equal degree; and the better this enforces a law of nature, while taxes violates it".-1

In many ways taking money from one person to fund a government healthcare program is a wealth redistribution. Stealing from one man the fruits of his labor to give to someone whose sweat was not in it. It's hard to talk about this without making Romney's infamous "47%" mistake. Romney should have chosen his words more carefully, but it is a real and growing problem. It is likely that, by the time you have read this book, I will have to have been one of those 47%ers because of unemployment insurance. To me, however, there is serious shame in it. It is not mine nor my employer's fault. Business just dried up. I do know who to blame though, and this is where it's going to get complicated, so bear with me a little.

There is a direct correlation between government spending and the value of the dollar. With the government debt ever increasing, more money is being printed to cover the cost of all these programs, many of which are unnecessary luxuries as I have mentioned previously. Much of the spending is designed to share spoils which benefit specific special interests who supported the party or candidate in question. As more is printed, the value of each dollar on the market decreases. This means it takes more dollars to do fewer things. More dollars buy less food, gas, pay less bills etc.

This also makes those government programs perpetually more expensive. Therefore, a problem which necessitates printing devalues the dollar, which necessitates more printing. Still with me? Okay. This is the root cause of inflation. The government then must start to pay for the interest on these debts being accrued so, naturally, they want to collect more taxes which leaves you with fewer dollars to do even less with. Meanwhile, they are simultaneously devaluing what dollars you have left. Stated differently; the government is screwing you in two ways now.

While inflation goes up the wealth disparity increases. When taxes go up, the wealth disparity increases because the rich have enough in investments to offset inflation. The increase in income taxes causes the rich to bank what they have and stall expansion of their economic endeavors. This means there's less money to invest in you... which means you don't get your raise, promotion, or even the job in the first place. Now you have less money, which is less valuable, that can afford you less of a quality lifestyle.

The way to reverse this is scary, but if you want to put an end to the death spiral we've put ourselves into, it involves very real spending cuts and I mean by the trillions. Ending programs which are superfluous, ending entitlement programs which are not actually helping people out of poverty (whatever that is in America) and reforming the big three entitlements to make them affordable. I'd like to see them gone. I will, however, cede to you that is an extreme position by modern political measurements (though it is moderate by Jeffersonian standards.) If I were to run for office, I would not seek the elimination of Medicare, Medicaid and Social Security Insurance, but we do have to reform them.

I like the idea of raising the retirement age to 70, I know it sucks, but if you want things affordable again we must do this or face perpetual rape at the grocery store. These programs were not designed to carry people through ten or twenty years. At their inception most people lived to about 65 or so. Now folks are reaching 80, or even 100. This is causing serious strain on the public system. Left unchanged, payroll taxes will have to be raised otherwise, and you will feel that pinch when food costs are raised by the grocery store to make up the lost revenue.

I also like turning Medicare and Medicaid over to the states. The States are much more local and have the ability to better facilitate the next reform I like which is means testing. While I am not a fan of taking from one to support another, since these programs do that anyway, we may as well save ourselves some money by not enabling people who don't need the programs to use them. We should also means and drug test for food stamps which should also be facilitated by the states, as should unemployment insurance.

With that said, none of these reforms should even be discussed before Obamacare is repealed. Republicans and Independents alike hate this monstrosity, but just accepting it and promising to manage it better will only ensure the nation's debt problem is never solved. I want see the national debt dealt with the way Democrat Andrew Jackson did, by eliminating it completely.

The next step is that a free market based alternative to our social programs are needed. For instance, people should be able to buy into an unemployment insurance that would cover a reasonable amount of unemployment, based on the customer's contributions, anywhere from a couple weeks to a couple months and your rates of compensation can vary based on what you pay. The program could offer 100% of your income for a period of time in the event you are unexpectedly unemployed, again within reason. Then the insurance company could reduce the amount the laid off employee gets over time until the plan dries up, but if you get yourself fired you should be SOL. This would be much better than the current plan offered by Uncle Sam, which often doesn't even provide a fraction of a laid off employee's income, has a ridiculously long wait time and also doesn't come regularly enough and doesn't last long enough in some cases.

Although, some states go as much as ninety-nine weeks, which is probably too long.

Similarly, a free market based alternative to Social Security ought to be introduced. Wait, it has. It's called 401k and frankly I can't direct my money there because I am forced into financially stagnant programs that don't build equity, such as Social Security. The program should allow me out if I would rather invest my money elsewhere, it should be my choice. What's wrong with letting me choose?

These changes will help reduce the strain on the system, making taking care of those who need the programs a lot easier and ensuring the sustainability of these programs. Unfortunately, if you propose these ideas to a Democrat, they'll make a video featuring you tossing a grandma off a cliff, or accuse you of wanting to kill women.

These steps will put us on the path to serious debt reduction. Now, want to eliminate it completely? Here's the compromise part the right won't like: total elimination of all tax deductions. This is a defacto tax increase on everyone, but then everyone should pay their fair share, right Mr President?

Then the compromise the left won't like: to make this move so it is not crippling, we then cut the tax rates to two brackets: 10% for people making less than 250,000 a year and 25% for those making more. The eventual goal is the elimination of the income tax, but first we have to pay off the national debt. This does hit the poor, but even God asks 10%, and it's really not all that much. I think I pay some 15% or so, I don't know which bracket I'm in, but whatever it is I'm in the "soak him every two weeks then also another grand at the end of the year" bracket. The current tax system is cumbersome and confusing, this will simplify it by eliminating tax evasion (legal or otherwise) and nearly flattening the tax so we are treated nearly uniformly. This is ideal because I do believe in *legal equality.* Legal equality is a vastly superior ideology to *Social Justice,* which uses the force of law to divide people into groups and treat them unequally. This legal equality based tax program can fit on half a page, as opposed to the Social Justice inspired 76,000 page monstrosity we have now.

These taxes should be used exclusively to manage programs deemed absolutely necessary, defense and paying OFF the national debt. *Nothing else.*

Now here's the real killer, and this will temporarily hurt the economy, but it is necessary to reduce the money supply. We must raise interest rates. Damn! Now I'll never get elected. We should not raise them to oppressive levels, but it's been kept artificially at almost 0% by the federal reserve for quite some time and all that extra money that's been printed is hurting the value of the dollar, as this money is reigned in, it must be destroyed by the federal reserve. I think a 5% rate would not be too devastating and again it should be temporary. Doing this will increase the value of the remaining dollars in the market, thus increasing the value of your wage, meaning you can do more with fewer dollars.

Bankers will whine that this is deflation and it's harmful to them and Wall Street, but why should I give a fig about banks and Wall Street? I care about putting food on my table! So don't listen to the naysayers and don't let them scare you by calling this deflation. It's a necessary *market correction.* If we do this, prices will come down and the value of your wage will go up. Does that sound bad to you? This will hit Wall Street, but after about two years things will boom and economic activity will explode. How do I know? Ever hear of the depression of the 1920s? No? It was the roaring twenties right? It was awesome! This is what Warren G Harding began and Calvin Coolidge finished.

Democrats like to blame the roaring 20s for the later great depression, but let's straighten out a few fantasies of theirs shall we? Calvin Coolidge was not a Progressive President, he ran an administration that went in the opposite direction. However, Herbert Hoover, his successor, *was* a Progressive and implemented Progressive policies. The most damaging Hoover Policy was the Smoot-Hawley Tariff, which drastically increased the tax on imported goods making them more expensive. So naturally, people quit buying imports and so the market crashed. Then we tried to solve a problem caused by a Progressive Republican by electing a Progressive Democrat, Franklin Delano Roosevelt, who just doubled down on Hoover's policies (kinda like how Obama just doubled down on Bush's). We seem to make this mistake a lot... but the good news is there is an out! We just have to do everything I mentioned previously and one more thing.

We have to pay off our own debt as individuals. We didn't do this step in the 1920s which became part of the problem in the 30s... This will also increase our disposable income. When our disposable income increases, our ability to accumulate that wealth (or in other words, save) will increase and your boss will be a lot more open to investing more in you. This opens up possibilities of promotions, or pay increases which will add even more disposable income to your wallet. The rich will also be much less afraid to spend their money and invest it, which means they'll have less tucked away in their banks and guess what happens to the income gap when we have more to save and the rich are spending more? Yup, that's right, it begins to close.

Chapter 3 references-

1-The Writings of Thomas Jefferson Albert Ellery Bergh ed. Vol. 14:466 (1816)

Chapter 4: Government's Job Is Not Wealth Redistribution.

Jefferson once bemoaned the fact that it is "…a cruel fate that a rich country cannot long be a free one…"-1. It's a lament that I fear has roots in the simple truth that where there is wealth, arrogance and lust for power inevitably becomes a part of the equation. Democrats see this in corporations, but the irony is that they fail to see it in themselves, let alone in the government. As a result the Democrats see their role in government as trying to balance everyone out financially. The vast majority of our leviathan government is welfare programs, but it isn't working. People aren't becoming more equal, it's just getting harder to get rich. It's getting harder for the McDonald's employee to create his own burger joint to compete in the market. I don't know if you know this but Dave Thomas, the founder of Wendy's, was originally a chef for KFC, but then he came up with an idea for "old fashioned burgers" and set about chasing after his dream. It didn't used to be impossible for that to happen.

Today, if you want to start a business, you have to begin with a mountain of paper work and wade your way through the suspicious eyes of the IRS. You have millions of regulations to wade through as well. It's an expensive and time consuming process, which discourages most people and forces them to accept their lot in life. We've already talked about how this impacts the income gap, but it is important to point out that although Jefferson was aware of the greed and corruption of corporations, his solution to the problem was essentially to maintain the freedom of the individual, and organizations of individuals working together for a common purpose, or an incorporation, to pursue their interests and compete. The Founding Fathers did not set up a system of wealth redistribution; competition would keep the rich in check. These mechanisms didn't enter the equation until the Progressive era of the 20th century, which Republicans have wanted to scale back, but have been too afraid to.

Morally speaking, the idea of wealth redistribution is reprehensible, and it's not new. It's been around since the dawn of time and quite frankly, it is one method of making a slave out of an individual. Now, taxes are a necessary evil, but there comes a point where enough is enough. I live in Utah where the spineless rule, so we have very heavy taxes here, albeit a lower income tax rate. We're in a pickle because we have high property taxes, moderate sales taxes, income tax, payroll tax, and the federal income tax. Oh, and in some areas our Unified Police Department charges a Progressive service fee on top of everything else. We are taxed enough already here, but if you say so the Salt Lake Tribune will call you an extremist. We have a Progressive Healthcare exchange, they were working on it before Obama Care. Also, 100% of our income tax, and a huge chunk or our property tax, funds our Progressive education system. Now, bear in mind I am poor. By the time all the taxes are done with me, more than half my income is eaten by the greed of government so that they can pay for someone else to have services they would likely be able to pay for themselves, if the government would just stay the heck out of our wallets. Ironically, services I am having a hard time getting when I need them, so I don't exactly feel like I am getting a return on this investment I am being forced into.

Remember I said that charity is one of our most noble aspirations next to liberty, but charity is voluntary, not government force. I have a problem with the philosophy of altruism for this reason. I look at how much better my life would be if I could just be allowed to keep my money, but because of altruism (an obsessive compulsive *need* to engage in helping the poor at someone else's expense rather than your own) it's harder for me to engage in charity. How do I give my 10% when 50% is already gone, taken by force not by my choice?

What I am about to suggest here is very controversial in Utah and will ensure that no Republican will ever elect me to anything ever again, I think states like Florida have the best solution for paying for education. Ready for it? Let's ditch the state income tax and install a state lottery. Yes, the poor buy lots of lottery tickets when they should buy food, but right now I have to drive to Idaho to buy them, and that's a lot of gas! Here's the deal, don't tell me you don't want a lottery because you are worried about how it will hurt the poor, when you are willing to take money out of their paychecks before they even get it, and charge them an arm and a leg just for owning a house or a car! The fact is that Florida has this right because they have developed a system of collecting state funding that is *voluntary,* and if you can collect funds for the state through voluntary measures, that is within the confines of natural law, whereas a tax, as we mentioned previously, violates it.

That is the entire method by which government can honorably acquire the means for whatever ends it desires. I've also argued for a marginal Fair Tax to replace the 16th amendment previously, this is the moral argument for it. If a tax is attached to consumption, then it is collected in a voluntary transaction. However, if it is taken by force, out of a pay check, it is stealing the fruits of one's labors much as the Democrats did to the African Americans in the early days on the United States.

When the fruits of your labors are taken from you without your consent, what else could it be but slavery? Especially when you have so much being taken! A lot of these individual taxes seem small, it's when you add them all up you see how you're getting screwed. While you fret about this program or that being shut down, ask yourself this question: what could you afford if you didn't have to worry about the difference between gross and net? Just imagine for a second, a full paycheck... A full paycheck! Then the fruits of your labors are yours and yours alone. You want to help the poor? Go right ahead! If you want to fund education, buy a lotto ticket. It seems callous, but it is working in other states, and it has been working better than what we've been doing here in Utah.

The thing is that taxes collected should be voluntary. Taxes collected in any other way its theft and theft is immoral. America needs to embrace volunteerism rather than altruism. Trust me, people's lives will get a lot better a lot quicker if they can keep their own money. Moreover, if you Democrats and Progressive Republicans agree to stay out of my wallet, then my compromise to you is that I will stay out of your bedroom, but we'll get to that later.

Ultimately, the government's role is not to provide equal things at the expense of only a few. There is a uniformity clause to the Constitution, which is always ignored, that is supposed to ensure everyone is treated exactly the same by the law regardless of class, creed or race. In order to ensure equality under the law in our society, we must ensure that the law does not treat anyone different regardless of race, creed or income. Our current welfare state *does* discriminate. We've just convinced ourselves that hate is okay... if it's directed at the rich (or Christians, and especially rich Christians.) Our country's past failings have been a direct result of failing to live up to that higher ideal of equality under the law. Should the government want to get into those kinds of redistributive services, then it must fund them only by voluntary measures.

Chapter 4 references

1- The Writings of Thomas Jefferson Albert Ellery Bergh ed. Vol. 17:162 (1787)

Chapter 5: Denying The Right To Life And Being Moronic When Defending It

In 2010, I had one candidate who I knew in my heart was destined for great things. Those of you who know me know who that candidate was. Everyone else I supported was, for me, about getting the best candidate possible and then getting them elected. The one I felt had a destiny for greatness lost, though I still have a hunch great things are on their way from him. He may have lost his race but perhaps other avenues will open for him.

Incidentally, that candidate never let on that he felt a call from destiny. If he did, he kept it to himself, however he was rare among Conservatives... If there is one complaint I *do* have about Conservatives, is that they tend to look at themselves as *"the Hero of Destiny."* They all look at politics as if they have donned the green tunic and cap, have just entered the Temple of Time and the election is the fulfillment of their destiny, as they draw forth the coveted Master Sword and set about on their quest to turn it into the Sword of Evil's Bane, before our mad dash to confront the evil Gannondorf. We on the Right can be a bunch of dorks, and that lack of humility can cause all kinds of irreparable damage during an election.

That ego problem pales in comparison to the narcissism we've seen from Obama and the radical extremists who have hijacked the Democratic party in the last ten years, but they have the media to cover for them. Often times our ego stops us from doing the right things for the party, or at least articulating our message correctly. We tend to shun the idea that we should put the needs of the party ahead of ourselves. Frankly, most of the time, this is a good thing. There are lines in the sand which must be drawn. Ron Paul seldom backed down, and now almost everything he has stood for has been implemented into the party platform in some fashion or another. There are times a hard choice has to be made and we should stand when it is right, but when something is so wrong it could actually harm the cause of liberty, one should recognize the need to step aside and let someone else give it ago. This is where our egos can get in the way.

Rep. Todd Akin's comments on "legitimate rape" were inexcusable. Not only were they scientifically unfounded assertions, but they do not represent the feelings of *any* faction of the GOP. Stated differently, no Republican feels the way he does. He is clearly insane. Worse, he's clearly not that bright. Nevertheless, Akin's comments were used as an albatross to hang around all of our necks. The right to life is a great argument to make and yes, the left loves to complicate things by tossing out nuanced arguments over exceptions. Every rule has an exception and our society has embraced exceptions for rape, incest or when the health of the mother is at risk. That is the Republican, also Mormon for that matter, view of things.

I think I know what Akin was trying to say, but he should have said it this way, "My wife and I could not hold an unborn child responsible for the crimes of its father, if it happened to my wife. We would raise that child as our own, but that is our personal view of things, and not reflective of the party at large. I personally believe that man is punished for their own sins and not for their father's transgressions. Once again, that view is not reflective of the party at large and I would not seek to change the accepted exceptions." I know this feeling well because after 8 years of an uphill battle with my wife's complex fertility issues and 8 years of not being able to have a child, we have developed a rather nuanced view. We desperately want a child, but adoption, I am sorry to say, is too expensive. It's not fair that there are so many children being thrown away, when there are people like us who would love to have them. This issue requires careful explanation in today's erratic, hyper-emotional and political world. Generally speaking, if it can't fit on a bumper sticker, don't bother. My anti-abortion view cannot fit on a bumper sticker, neither could Akin's, but where I can couch mine in carefully crafted nuance based on personal experience, Akin, reached out to medical journals from the stone age to rationalize his stance, and hurt the entire party in the process.

The media had already manufactured the fictional narrative that Republicans were waging some sort of insidious war on women. Before Akin's comments, they had no evidence to support their absurd claims, afterward they had all the proof they needed. Many in the party pushed for Akin to step down, but he didn't back down despite polling indicating a ten point shift from a leans Republican Senate seat to a safe Democrat seat. Now, Akin worked hard to defeat two Tea Party candidates, John Brunner and Sarah Steelman. When he beat them, the Tea Party walked away from that race. Then Akin spoke up on abortion and blew it. Think about this for a minute, from leans Republican all the way to *safe* Democrat. Romney, thankfully still won the state of Missouri, but we should have had that senate seat too. And now to piss off the moderates, I dare venture to say that Tea Partier, Sarah Steelman, would have won it for us. The GOP *should have* taken action to force Akin out. Ann Coulter proposed grabbing someone like Kit Bond, former Governor and Senator from MO, and running them in an all-out write in campaign. We were going to lose that seat with Akin anyway. I think Coulter had a valid point. Claire McCaskill isn't very popular, and before Akin's comments she was losing by ten points, after she won handedly.

Ann Coulter wasn't the only one to throw her voice in the ring asking for the MO GOP to do a write in campaign with someone viable. The Romney campaign moved quickly to put distance between themselves and the Akin camp. Karl Rove, who had sunk millions of dollars into helping Akin beat the oh so evil Tea Party candidates, pulled all further financial contributions to the Akin campaign. I also added my voice to the mix, though I cede the point *I'm just a nobody from Tooele.* Even so, it is important that our party do something about this when it happens in the future, and quick. Yes there's a double standard in the media. Yes, Democrats get away with garbage like this all the time. Yes, if you want to see real misogyny, one need only look at how the Democrats and their collaborators in the news media have treated SE Cupp, Ann Coulter, Michelle Bachman, Sarah Palin, Bristol Palin, Nikki Haley, the list goes on for miles... but even so, the double standard exists because, unlike

Democrats, WE HAVE STANDARDS. Thus we ought to insist that our standard bearers accurately reflect our world views.

Since Akin's messiah complex didn't let him see the need to step aside, we ought to have forced his hand. Since we couldn't, then Ann Coulter was right, a write in campaign was necessary. We cannot afford to keep losing seats because our candidates can't articulate our values correctly. Akin wasn't the Tea Party guy anyway, contrary to the myth now being sewn by the establishment who went out of their way to help beat the Tea Party candidates Sarah Steelman and John Brunner. Akin was the result of an open primary where Democrats could vote on who our candidate would be.

This is another example of why Utah's closed primaries are superior to other state's open primaries. Open primaries allow for Democrats to select the easiest Republican to beat. Missouri's GOP might also want to consider their election process and ask if it could be amended to prevent morons like Akin from getting the candidacy by adopting closed primaries. They may even want to consider a system similar to Utah's Neighborhood Caucus system, which, despite the fantasies of the far left loons that write the SLTRIB, does a great job of weeding out the crazies as well as the spineless weaklings.

Now I must discuss Tea Party Candidate, Richard Murdoch, who beat a 36 year GOP incumbent in the 2012 primary, but lost the general election due to a controversy surrounding his thoughts on abortion. I don't think it error to say that all life is a gift from God. It's a legitimate religiously founded position to take. This was a situation where we should have circled the wagons, because when you look at that case, it was pretty clear the Democrats were playing word games, making it seem like he had said something infinitely worse than what was said. What he really said was life is a gift from God, generally speaking. I do agree how he said it was poorly phrased, but his comments were not malicious. If life isn't a gift from God, then why are we using the Sandy Hook Tragedy as justification for taking away our guns? Either life is sacred or its not.

Remember what Ayn Rand taught us, "There are no contradictions, where one occurs check your premises. You will find one of them is wrong." So either life is sacred, as I said, and all life should be protected, or none of it is. If it is not sacred, then why bother mourning the loss of innocent life at all? But here's a Democratic lead contradiction in play. If it's a defense of life still in the womb it's a mass of tissue not worth arguing about. Yet, if it exists outside the womb, it's a prop for whatever political agenda they are pushing, unless you're Dr Kermit Gosnell who thinks a pair of scissors can solve any child-related problem. This is the kind of guy who deserves to burn in hell for what he has done, cutting the spines of new born infants with a pair of shears and calling it an abortion. Yet, the media circled the wagons around him, until he was found guilty of infanticide. This is the same media who crucified the guy who said all life is a gift from God.

It's sick double standard really, but it is what it is. Which is why when someone says life is a gift from God we shouldn't be afraid to stand with them. However, when someone says that a woman's body can shut down a "legitimate rape", we should run him out of town with pitchforks and torches. One is a legitimate religious belief, the other is blatant stupidity. We can tolerate, at least, the former but should depose the latter.

From a religious standpoint, Murdochs view is not inconsistent with the Bible where Jesus warned: "It were better for him that a millstone were hanged about his neck, and he cast into the sea, than that he should offend one of these little ones." (Luke 17:2). This more than suggests that God is more than a little protective of children. We ought to be as well as there is nothing more precious. I should know, my wife and can't have one.

Sadly, our society has so lost its way that it is an extreme position to say that there should be no abortions. It's sad, but even the LDS church, and indeed most churches, have come to accept the health/rape/incest exceptions and no Republican should allow themselves to be duped into saying otherwise. This exception wins, and it's the exception that society had already accepted, but we now need to be prepared to re-sell this argument, thanks to Akin and the misrepresented words of Murdoch. The more Christian of us may cringe at the thought, but it is a political reality. This matter was settled a long time ago and the Democrats know it. Why do you think their new argument was the false claim that the GOP wanted to take away contraception? A false premise, by the way.

The phony war on women won the election, in part, by scaring people about something that no one was talking about. Sadly, we did nothing to dismiss this silliness... well I did, by asking GOP candidates about this directly when I had the chance to interview them. Everyone I interviewed thought the whole matter was silly. (You can see these interviews on my You Tube Page The Unapologetic Apologist. Though none of the candidates I interviewed won.) Still, I was blown away by the way this matter was simply dismissed, instead of addressed.

Here is the deal folks: The GOP has no more desire to be inside a woman's womb than to eat shards of broken glass. The fact of the matter is that we honestly don't care what you do in your bedroom, never have. We only care when a child is needlessly and senselessly murdered as a means of very expensive and barbaric birth control. Much rather, would we that you *take* your damn contraception and prevent it…

Except that Catholics don't believe in contraception and should not be forced to pay for yours, and that is exactly what Obama had done. He ordered, via mandate, that contraception be covered, even by institutions morally opposed to such. So now, thanks to Tyrannosaurus Barack-Rex, the government has the power to force church based institutions to act against their conscious. It was THAT MANDATE that the GOP was opposed to, for the very same reasons you are opposed to us taking tax money to pay for wars for oil. You are being forced to act against your conscious.

The truth about contraception is that mostly, we don't care, but Sandra Fluck lied about its costs, and grossly exaggerated it's necessity. It doesn't cost $3,000 a year. When my wife was on it, it cost us $20 a month and a grand total of $240 a year. Moreover, condoms cost even less. I don't care what goes on in your bedroom, but there's no reason I should be made to pay for it.

So the great compromise here is two part:

1) Health, rape incest exceptions, but otherwise a child has the right to his or her life, liberty and property and should not be denied any of the aforementioned without due process.

2) I don't care what you do in your bedroom or what you put in your womb, it's the last place I'd want to be for sure. But it is awfully rotten of you to expect that I should pay for your leisurely activities. Stay out of my wallet and I will stay out of your bedroom.

Chapter 6: Political Props

If there is one thing I cannot stomach, it is the way that politicians use props to distract us. Logic and reason should guide our politicians, but that isn't the way it usually works. Bush used an irrational fear of terrorism, though to be fair, it was a much more generic terror than portrayed. He was far from anti-Muslim. Obama, meanwhile, taps into people's fear and emotions about wealth and race.

Let's face it, the numbers did not bode well for Obama. Real unemployment has stayed at about 14-15% (that's the U6 number in the Department of Labor statistics that the media likes to avoid.) Some two million jobs evaporated since Obama took office. The labor force participation rate was down, but the media kept trying to convince you unemployment is getting better through a bit of chicanery. You see, the Department of Labor Statistics tracks unemployment in a few different ways. The number they give you, the U3 number, does not include people who no longer qualify for unemployment insurance, nor does it count people who have given up looking for work. The resulting number from that fudged math will go down regardless of whether or not people are actually finding work. The U6 number is the number that should have been watched because it tells the real story, counting everyone who isn't working.

The economy isn't healthy. Right after the election, the U3 number shot right back up from 7.7% to 7.8%. Incidentally, this was the same number the U3 rate was when Obama took office. Since then, unemployment dropped down to 7.7% again, but the labor force participation rate has dropped from 65% to 63% in the same time, a record low. There is no logical reason Obama should have been re-elected, and don't blame Romney's 47% comment. The comment may have been in artfully said, but the point was sound. About 47% of this nation, and now more than that, receive more in their tax refunds than they pay in, or are on some sort of government program, though I missed the memo on how to do that. Romney was acknowledging that these folks may not be reachable with the typical tax cut/regulation reduction arguments we tend to make. It was a logical, numbers based acknowledgement of a problem the GOP has, though it wouldn't be a problem if our politicians acted on numbers (logic) and not emotion.

Despite the innocuous nature of the 47% comments, people harped on them as a means to beat up on Romney. Here are the comments for your consumption:

> There are 47 percent of the people who will vote for the president no matter what. All right, there are 47 percent who are with him, who are dependent upon government, who believe that they are victims, who believe the government has a responsibility to care for them, who believe that they are entitled to health care, to food, to housing, to you-name-it. That that's an entitlement. And the government should give it to them. And they will vote for this president no matter what...

> These are people who pay no income tax. 47 percent of Americans pay no income tax. So our message of low taxes doesn't connect...

> And so my job is not to worry about those people. I'll never convince them that they should take personal responsibility and care for their lives.-1

True that some of these folks may be on Social Security and what have you, but it is a statistical fact. Where Romney errored was in the assumption that these folks want to be in that rut. I disagree with the close of the statement. I believe most *do* want to take personal responsibility, but are afraid to spread their wings because Obama keeps telling them they can't make it without him. "You didn't build that!" He said referring to entrepreneur's businesses, "someone else built that for you!" I don't believe people want to be dependent upon *givernment*, I know I don't.

As cold as Romney's statements may have been, one shouldn't interpret this as Romney "doesn't care" about 47% of the people. Look at the text again. If you remove your emotion from it, you can clearly see Romney is talking numbers. Romney was not an emotional guy. He's a very left brained (mathematical) moderate who was talking about statistics, not people. Perhaps that was the error of the statement, but to his defense, similar statistics are all abound in elections and I eat them like candy... and I eat A LOT of candy. The conventional wisdom is that you'll have 40% that vote Democrat no matter what and 40% who vote Republican no matter what. Winning the election comes down to convincing the folks that make up that last 20%. As annoying as this is for the 40% of true believer Republicans and Democrats, it really does boil down to that 20% of fence sitters most of the time. Often times, about half the fence sitters go Democrat and the other half go Republican. As you can see, based on that statistical tendency, having around 47% defaulting to one side or another is a fair expectation. Romney's concern was that the low taxes argument the GOP always makes would not resonate with 47% of the people, so he had to focus on bring out the voters who would respond to his message. That is all! The 47% Romney was referring to are *Democrats*, or lean left, or are like Occupy Wall Street, pushing for greater dependency on the teat of government. Those folks are never going to vote Republican, and outreach to them is a fool's errand. That is all Romney meant. Though to be fair, I believe the Occupy folks represent an extremist, but vocal, minority within the Democratic party. Sadly the same minority who happen to control the leadership of their party, the media and academia.

Yet, after this comment was made it was non-stop 24-7 news: "Romney doesn't care about 47% of the people!" As you can see, it was a lie. Nowhere did Romney say "I don't care about 47% of the country." Nevertheless, you got distracted, didn't you? Even now, Republicans bash Romney for the 47% comments while making the same argument in the same breath. (I'm looking at you Colin "Obama can do no wrong" Powell!)

Or did you think the election was about birth control? I've already mentioned this as a diversionary tactic. No one should have bought into this but when you live in a world of sound bites and bumper stickers, it's often hard to discern fact from fantasy. Still, there is one distraction above all else that irks me in ways nothing else comes even close to. Quit using children as props!

Obama has gone to lengths I have never seen before... well, not without having to resort to Godwin's law and start pulling Hitler Youth Corps videos out... First, the "Obama's gonna lead us" song that came around the internet during his first election, then post-election the "Mmmm, mmm, Barack Hussein Obama" video. In both young Children who were too young to understand anything about politics, were used to sing Obama praises... literally... in a manner which was disturbingly messianic. While I normally refrain from using Godwin's law to further an argument, one cannot ignore the eerie similarities to Hitler Propaganda videos, perfectly illustrated here: https://www.youtube.com/watch?v=mOl-HE-6rS0. Next, Obama's crew filmed ads where Children were lecturing their parents about their need to trust their children's enlightened views and vote for Obama... I mean this is nonstop with this administration and it's creepy.

Ironically, Obama once declared that the families of politicians should be off limits. I agree, but that didn't stop the left from hammering Sarah Palin's family, even going so far as accusing her as using her newborn son, Trigg, as a prop during the 2008 Republican Convention. Look, it's one thing to have your family sitting or standing with you when you're accepting the nomination to a major position for a major political party, it's quite another to shield yourself with other people's children when promoting the disarming of law abiding citizens.

After the Sandy Hook incident Obama gave a lecture about how he must usurp power, take it away from you and I in the name of the greater good. He cushioned it by having children read letters they had allegedly written begging him, basically to take guns away. It's interesting that he does not have children read letters begging him to stop abortion, which kills more children every year than gun violence. The former is increasing every year and has killed 50 million unborn babies since Roe V Wade. The latter, you'll recall, has actually been in decline and has only been responsible for a few thousand incidents in the same time frame. This is nowhere near the kind of numbers abortion has reached.

Then the NRA responds by running an ad pointing out that Obama's kids get armed security but ours don't. It challenges the fairness of this and I think makes a great point. Jefferson once described his role as President as being one among equals. Today we treat our president as a king and that is a problem, but it was wrong to use Obama's kids to make that point. In fact, it's wrong to use anyone's kids.

Children are human beings, most of them are more concerned about where they're going to get their next chocolate bar than who the president is. I know, I was a kid once, and you can tell by looking at me I spent a lot of time looking for chocolate. As a kid, I did adore Ronald Reagan. I always got the impression that he was a nice old grandpa, and the fact that he sent my family Christmas cards, for reasons I never did figure out, reinforced this. But as a kid, I had no idea what was going on in the political arena, though Reagan, alongside Coolidge, remains my favorite contemporary president.

Most kids are going to like the President no matter what party he is. For kids, meeting the President is a great honor, but ninety-nine percent of them will be bored after five minutes of meeting him and ninety-nine percent of them are not informed enough to have written the letters they read without parental guidance. Ninety-nine percent of the kids he surrounded himself with on what I have come to call Usurpation Day will grow up with their faces permanently palmed in humiliation that they got used this way. I know. My mom did it to me... sort of...

I love my mom, don't get me wrong. However, this was one occasions I got used for a political agenda I am totally opposed to. I have been playing games since I was a kid. I've been working since I was 15, so I could buy the games my mom banned... which was all of them. My parents respected personal property, so I knew if I bought the game systems and the games myself, they would leave them alone. That still didn't stop my mom's anti-gaming crusades.

I've been on computer writing since I was ten. Between that, and the old non-ergonomic game controllers we used to use, I developed Carpal Tunnel and "Nintendo Thumb." Never so bad as to need any more than a brace to keep it controlled, but my mom wrote letters to politicians and to the local newspapers, *in my name,* bashing games for causing my Carpal Tunnel... I actually tried to write letters to follow up and correct the record and let everyone know what had happened, and that my mother's views on games did not represent mine. Unfortunately, no one printed my retraction. My mom meant well. She was concerned about my wrists, but I felt like I got used as a prop, and no one was interested in what I really had to say which was... But I love games!

There was a kid a few years ago, Jonathan Krohn. I think he was twelve. He wrote this brilliant book called *Defining Conservatism*. Fast forward to present day, guess what? He's a Liberal now. And here Huckabee had hoped the kid would be President someday. I bought his book, it was really good! It's out of print now and in storage, but I bring him up because the book I read could not have been written by a twelve year old. It was brilliant. I mean, it was really brilliant. Too brilliant for someone with the maturity level of a twelve year old to have written, and the fact that he now vigorously denounces that ideology is indicative that the feelings and logic of his book were clearly not his own. The energy he puts into denouncing Conservatism now suggests strong parental force may have played a part in his book, much as force played a role in the letter to the editor of the Tooele Transcript Bulletin, denouncing video games by Daniel A. Moir, a big fat gamer.

The fact of the matter is that it's wrong to use kids for politics. My niece, Jaq, has begged me to film her reporting the news, but she's only nine. I want her to relay the news the way she feels about it, not just regurgitate what she hears me, my wife or her mother say. We're all simpatico on the issues now, but I believe she needs to grow up and make up her own mind about things, not to be goaded into taking a stand she may disagree with in a few years. Maybe she'll come to me at age 18 and demand I give her a news show for You Tube. Lord knows she pesters me about this already, but at least when she is 18, I can have more confidence that her opinions will be purely her own and not just an echo of mine.

She often asks me what she should think about the issues, I respond to her as Jefferson responded to his nephew; "Question boldly the very existence of God, for if there be a God, surely he would rather *honest* questions to cold hearted fear." And ask questions she does, which drives her biological father (a Democrat) nuts... But nevertheless children must be allowed to learn and grow on their own, especially so that *reason,* rather than crass emotion, can prevail in their minds. We do them a great disservice dictating what to think, rather than teaching them how to learn for themselves.

Moreover, when children are used in politics, it often distracts from the fact that whoever is using the kids is trying to draw attention away from the fact that they are taking away some freedom or another. Regardless of their emotional words, when you remove the emotion from it, their message more often than not is, "Put these chains on! It'll be good for you! And besides, think of the children!"

Chapter 6 references:

1-Jumping the Gun of Romney '47%' video, Brendan Nyhan 9-18-12 http://www.cjr.org/united_states_project/jumping_the_gun_on_the_romney.php ?page=all accessed 1-17-13

Chapter 7: To Rush Limbaugh with Apologies.

Kids don't truly understand politics, I mean at all. Had, I when I was younger, I probably would not have been such a fan of Disney's Dinosaurs, remember? Not the Mama! We all remember Baby Sinclair, but for that adorable pink baby whacking his dad with a frying pan, not its extremely radical leftist preachiness. As a youngin' I never could understand why the series was so short lived. As an adult, I learned real fast by re-watching the series. People don't like politically preachy entertainment, and yet down the throats of our kids it goes, even though they are only laughing because someone is getting hit on the head with a frying pan. The kids aren't getting the tree-hugging brain washing that is happening.

As further proof that our kids shouldn't be targeted by the political class, allow me put forward some more personal experience. I remember around the same time Disney's Dinosaurs was on, Rush Limbaugh had a TV show, give or take a few years. I'm too lazy to Google it. Both shows were highly political, but I didn't get that either one was political. I only watched Rush because sometimes he would tell a funny joke about Bill Clinton. The rest of it went right over my head, and since Rush wasn't hitting anyone on the head with a frying pan, my attention to his message was nil. Thus, when the media started to berate him I did too... out of ignorance. I had an art teacher who would make a regular point to complain about him. When I got into Utah politics, everyone told me not to listen to Rush. He was a nut, he didn't represent the so called "mainstream." There were a lot of other names he was subjected to. I was told to listen to local radio host, Doug Wright, instead. I did at first, but I found Mister Wright didn't have the appreciate for the Conservative and Libertarian Grass Roots activists I felt they deserved. It is true that Doug Wright outpaces Rush in Utah's local ratings, but I began to feel lonely listening to him. It seemed odd to me that he didn't seem to appreciate that in order to keep the engine of a Democratic-Republic running smoothly, once in a while you have to change the oil.

That is what I would tell Bennett supporters when asked why I was backing his ousting... Still the local guy regularly expressed that people like me are nuts, so I decided to check in with Rush even though, as a kid, I had thought I didn't like him and as a tween I avoided him because I was told he was nuts. Suddenly, what I could never grasp as a ten year old made sense as a thirty-year old. Not only that, but Rush had an appreciation of the Grass Roots activists that the local guy didn't seem to have.

I, therefore, would like to start this chapter on apologies with an apology to Rush Limbaugh. I learned that the reason for his apparent abrasiveness isn't because he's a mean guy. In fact he has a heart of gold. It's because he is so hard of hearing he requires a hearing implant just to get by, so he can't hear. When he is being boastful he's actually just being sarcastic. Moreover, he is *always* taken out of context to make him say something he didn't say. Therefore the news media owes him an apology.

In example, the Sandra Fluck fiasco. I was listening that day. Sandra Fluck was brought in by Nancy Pelosi as a witness against the GOP's attempt to moderate Obama's extreme mandate, which required the Catholic Church to supply contraception to its employees, even though it violates key tenants if their faith. Sandra gave what is a mathematically bogus testimony, claiming that the contraception mandate was needed because she had to pay $3,000 a year for it. Well, anyone whose actually used contraception knows that is a mathematical impossibility. It's dirt cheap! To paraphrase Obama, Rush wasn't being partisan, he wasn't being stubborn, he was using simple math. He calculated that since the pill costs only about $20 a month or $240 a year, Ms. Fluck cannot possibly be spending the absurd amount of money on contraception she was claiming, unless she was doing it a lot more than the average Joe (or Jane, take your pick.) Ultimately, he said that the only way it was possible for her to spend that kind of money on contraception, unless she were a s*(t, and her demanding we pay for her sexual activities must make her a prostitute.

Now keep in mind, Ed Schultz had referred to Laura Ingram, a happily married woman, with children and an an active Christian, as the same words and there was silence from the media. No one cared when Bill Maher referred to Sarah Palin as the same and then one upped it calling her a c*^t. No one cared when Hustler photo shopped SE Cupp with a phallic in her mouth. Not a peep. Yet, when Rush Limbaugh questions a left wing kook on her math and uses the term as an expression of her obvious excesses, embellishments and ridiculous demands that we be made to pay for it all, the whole world fell into a tailspin.

It would be nice if we could get past all the name calling that goes on in politics, but I would flip that on the Democrats and demand that they stop calling our women sluts, skanks, whores, or even going so far as to suggest that our Ann Coulter is actually a man. I would further demand that they stop calling the Tea Party *extreme,* or anyone who wants to see our nation solvent radical, or anyone who believes in Jeffersonian Republicanism a racist.

As an interesting anecdote, the Democrats came from the Tertium Quids, a merging of the old Federalists with the Southern pro-slavery factions of the original Republican Party. They would break off to form the Democratic Party with a pro-slavery agenda. It was the Democrats who created the KKK and the Democrats who brought us Jim Crowe. Only through the dishonest manipulation of education and media do we somehow have the descendants of the Northern National Republicans, you know, the ***abolitionists***, getting labeled "racist." It is unbelievable to me, but they act as if we would totally agree with everything Obama has done but for the fact that he is black. I face palm every time I hear that ridiculous argument.

While it is true that there are a small handful of racists and misogynists and anti-(insert random group) radicals in every movement, the majority of the left and right are *both* ready to move beyond identity politics and name calling. But in the last almost decade that I have paid attention to politics, I've seen an endless barrage of insults and name calling from the left. Yet the minute someone on the Right calls them out on it, or returns fire for fire, the media pitches a fit.

Take the case of former Florida Rep. Allen West (R). He dared to suggest that

DNC Chair Debbie Wasserman Schultz wasn't a lady, an old school way of insinuating she's impolite. But this was in response to the fact that she had staged an anti-tea party rally in front of his office in Florida, and hadn't exactly been respectful in addressing him on the floor of Congress. She had used clever phrases while referencing West and the Tea Party which included swastikas, Nazi, Hitler, you know, the usual dribble (never mind that Nazi = National *SOCIALIST*). At any rate West replied to her behavior thusly:

> Look, Debbie, I understand that after I departed the House floor you directed your floor speech comments directly towards me. Let me make myself perfectly clear, you want a personal fight, I am happy to oblige. You are the most vile, unprofessional, and despicable member of the US House of Representatives. If you have something to say to me, stop being a coward and say it to my face, otherwise, shut the heck up. Focus on your own congressional district!

> I am bringing your actions today to our Majority Leader and Majority Whip and from this time forward, understand that I shall defend myself forthright against your heinous characterless behavior......which dates back to the disgusting protest you ordered at my campaign hqs, October 2010 in Deerfield Beach.

> You have proven repeatedly that you are not a Lady, therefore, shall not be afforded due respect from me!

Steadfast and Loyal

Congressman Allen B West (R-FL)

Debbie Wasserman Schultz is exactly everything that's wrong with the Democratic party, anyone who goes off on an imagined war on women, makes baseless allegations that the GOP are refusing to compromise, and are only trying to protect tax cuts for the rich, or of being Nazis, etc is trying to avoid the adult conversation these subjects deserve. Consequently I demand an apology from the following.

Debbie Wasserman Schultz

Clare McCaskill

John Kerry

Stephanie Cutter

Barack Obama

Nancy Pelosi

Maxine Waters

Harry Reid

If I keep listing names then this book will reach 300 pages too quickly. But on the right I want apologies from:

John McCain

Meghan McCain

Bob Bennett

Jeb Bush

John Huntsman Jr

Lindsay Graham

Paul Rowley

Olene Walker

Mike Leavitt

And also anyone else who said I wouldn't support Reagan because folks like me are "too extreme". Umm… can I just say, "what a load of crap?" Reagan did compromise, I'm not opposed to that at all, in fact I'm writing the book on it! However, compromise means that I get *something I want too.* Thus far, there has been no compromise, only capitulation to Obama and his extreme agenda, an agenda that by his own words is to, "fundamentally transform America." Not transform Washington, *you are the problem in his eyes,* and I have a problem with that. All I want is to preserve and restore America by changing Washington DC. I'm perfectly content to leave *you* alone, he's not. So who's the uncompromising extremist here?

Which sounds extreme to you? Fundamental transformation or preservation and restoration? Reagan's accomplishments cannot be ignored. He lowered taxes far more than he raised them. Taxes fell from some 70% for top earners to some 25-30% for top income earners. He deregulated where he could, and yes, he increased military spending, but this was a tactical move which forced Russia to overspend and collapse their own economy over time. The fact is that while I would not agree with Reagan 100% of the time, I know his agenda was the same as mine. This childish insult we wouldn't elect Reagan seems nonsensical, especially when it is coming from a group that proudly proclaims themselves as Progressive (which would be the antithesis of Reagan). It's another distraction, a means to avoid the very adult conversations we need to have.

By now these Progressives are demanding an apology from me, but I am of a mind to say the compromise for this nonsense is for them to apologize to us first and knock it off. Apologize to the American people for the distractions, and misdirection, and then to the GOP who has largely been the biggest target of this distractionary name calling. They need to apologize to Glenn Beck, whom I don't always agree with but has at least backed up his allegations with videos, and audio of the Democrats and Progressive Republicans saying exactly what he was accusing them of saying. Yet, he has been made a pariah in spite of the over whelming evidence he has supplied to make his case. Apologies need to be made to Sean Hannity, who really is our era's Sam Adams. He is a loud mouthed, but loveable, Son of Liberty who also backs up his claims with evidence. MSNBC has to edit things to make them something that they're not, like Romney's Wawa's comments, severely cut to make him appear out of touch. Or what they did to George Zimmerman, editing his 911 call to make him sound racist even though Zimmerman, it turns out, wasn't white himself. They're owed an apology too. Once that's all been done, then I'll apologize for comparing the left's ideology to the Communists, National Socialist German Worker's Party and 20th Century Progressives, and highlighting the disturbing similarities... even if that apology means I'd have to ignore history...

That's not to say that people on the right shouldn't apologize when they error, I am not defending Rush or West. Both could have found a better way to say what they had to say. Their rebuttals were very harsh, but that doesn't mean they didn't have a point. Both Wasserman Schultz and Fluck are kind of insane (can I say that and not be a misogynist?) And a straightjacket awaits Nancy Pelosi and Clare "they're trying to kill women" McCaskill at the end of their tenure, but there are fancier, more civilized ways of saying it... They may not be as fun though.

On the other hand it could be worse. Jefferson ran against Adams proclaiming him to be both a monarchist and a hermaphrodite... Though they did eventually kiss and make up, metaphorically speaking of course. And speaking of guys kissing...

Chapter Eight: The Fight Over Marriage...

Let's talk about this like adults. I am hard to label. To some I am a moderate, as I've been told I am weak on social issues. To others, I am extreme because I stand firm on liberty issues and I won't bend or compromise unless I get something I want in return. To many, my anti-tax stances make me Tea Party, but to still others, my willingness to compromise, no, prioritize issues, makes me not extreme enough. I walk into the gay marriage debate completely on the fence and persuadable and let me tell you why.

When I was in High School, a very close friend of mine blew the lid off my world when he disappeared for months on end without explanation. He was a very popular guy at school, so everyone was ecstatic when he returned. Everyone except one of my other close friends. My choir teacher (Yes I sing, shut up.) had to pause our lesson that day in the hopes of heading off what he feared would be a major blow out. Apparently, there was some news about our prodigal tenor that most of us hadn't heard. Our teacher tried to explain about tolerance and how sometimes people may go down roads we don't always agree with, but we need to love those people for who they are... Everyone was aghast. We already knew something was up when our prodigal singer finally stood up and put an end to all the guessing. He came out of the closet. My other friend blew a gasket, calling him all kinds of cruel names before punching a nearby wall so hard that it shattered his hand. When the dust settled my now out of the closet friend asked me if I would turn on him too. I've always been moderately religious, and I do hold religious views the bigoted Progressives might say are antiquated, but this was one of my best and most valued friendships at the time. I would not turn on that friend. Though we would eventually part ways over other political issues, this would not be one. He chose the path of the anti-religious, bigoted Progressive Leftist. Meanwhile, I chose the path of the Jeffersonian Republican.

I paid a heavy price for my loyalty. Being a 1st tenor myself, I've always had a higher pitched voice. I've always been dismissive of it, so did Lincoln, another of my favorite presidents. After I decided to stand by my friend when most didn't, people started coming after me. I was in art, I was in dance (honestly to try to meet chicks), I was in choir and I had a high pitched voice. Never mind the fact that I always walk with my chest up, head up high and my fists clenched (I got beat up a lot, it was a defensive posture) and I have never talked in that valley girl accent we so often hear... too many people assumed that the sum of these things, plus my rabid defense of my friend, meant I too must have been a closeted homosexual, which was simply never true. Bad enough that I received regular beatings because I read comic books, was admittedly socially awkward, my humor is more influenced by Mystery Science Theatre than the Simpsons and I sometimes spell theater as theatre... Now I had this to deal with. Everyone to the right of me wanted to mount my head to the wall next to the buffalo's (our school mascot). But it got worse.

Another friend, who was a flamboyant homosexual and everyone knew it, decided to come out, but it surprised no one. I'm sure he was ridiculed for it. I don't want to demean or challenge his experience, but whereas my first friend came out then tried to keep a low profile, this other friend came out and paraded it like he had singlehandedly just destroyed the Death Star. With my first friend, people went out of their way to target him as he tried to recapture some semblance of normalcy. This other friend, however, immediately began to try and get a petition to force the school to organize a gay club, paid for by the tax payer dollars. You know, for emotional support.

I wouldn't sign the petition on the grounds that I didn't feel it served an academic purpose and I did not feel it was a worthwhile use of tax payer dollars. Unfortunately, this rallied the left against me. Now, on top of being an artist with a high pitched voice, who was in a dance class (I swear to meet chicks), who obviously was only sticking up for his gay friend because he is secretly gay himself, I was also labeled a homophobic, religious zealot, bigot. Both sides would try to hit me with their cars, run me off the road, beat me up and make my life all kinds of miserable... and people wonder why I hate the Public School System... Oops, reason 195.3565 I'll never be elected. As a result of my personal experience, I believe I am one of a few in the State of Utah with a balanced view of this issue. Both sides have their victims and both sides have their bullies. I've been at the wrong end of both side's fists.

For every school yard bully beating up the gay kid, there's a Dan Savage (an entirely appropriate name) persecuting Christian youth for their deeply held religious beliefs. I generally hate Friedrich Nietzsche, but he did have this brilliant anecdote: "Whoever fights with monsters must see to it that in the process he does not become one himself. And if you spend long enough gazing into the abyss, you will find it is gazing back at you." This is a heart breaking comment because it is so true. It is the point that many of history's greatest villains have always missed. When you read history you always see this, it happened with Ceaser, it happened with Vlad III Dracula (yes he was real), it happened with Lenin, Hitler and Stalin. They all became the monsters they fought against. In the epic film *The Dark Knight*, Harvey Dent observed that, "you either die the hero, or you live long enough to see yourself become the villain." He then went on to become the villain. Truer words could not be spoken. It is why George Washington stepped down after two terms. It is why the United States term limited the President after FDR's four terms, look into what kind of monster he became in his last two terms. They don't talk about it in school, but America was clearly headed toward a dictatorship. People like Dan Savage need to be aware of this. I have observed countless You Tube videos of this guy doing "anti-bullying" presentations at schools, only to go on an anti-Christian tirade, in a public school! The man is out of control. Clearly, he found the abyss staring right back at him and liked it.

That said, I have been involved with Utah's political scene long enough to have talked to a lot of people on this issue. The left doesn't feel that we have the right to dictate our morality to them by force of government. The right is split. There is a segment that feels that they must regulate morality to slow the spread of blood diseases, though modern medicine and frankly condoms eliminate this argument. Most are just afraid that their religious rights will be squashed in the process of legalizing gay marriage.

For the LDS Church, homosexuality is not hated, nor do we encourage the persecution of homosexuals. To the contrary, we are to love them and be there for them as we would anybody else. While I cannot speak for the Church, I can say that it is atypical for homosexuality to be treated any differently than fornication or adultery. Why? It is our belief that sex is only acceptable in the confines of a loving monogamist marriage between a man and a woman. That is what the Bible teaches and what we, likewise, believe. To hold to those values is not hate. We understand that not everyone is going to share that world view. So why Proposition Eight?

Well the role of the LDS Church in Prop Eight, in my opinion, has been grossly exaggerated. We just happen to be on the Progressive's list of people okay to hate along with black conservatives, female conservatives, southerners, people who make more than $250,000 a year, white evangelicals and meat, no matter how tasty. The LDS population in California is a measly 2% of the total population and declining. Like most of the other Conservatives in California, Mormons are leaving en masse as the state continues to sink itself in massive debt and taxes. If you look at the numbers, it was the minority population (Blacks and Hispanics) who were the votes that put the gay marriage ban over the edge.-1

What I am about to say is purely conjecture, and I have no evidence to support it, but here's something I noticed. At the same time Prop Eight was going on in

California, a handful of States back east were also flirting with legalizing Gay Marriage. Yet the Church only focused it's anxieties on California. Prop Eight was an amendment to the State's Constitution, which would make a traditional marriage the only type recognized by the state. This step was taken because the Courts threw out a previous voter initiative, which merely made gay marriage against the law.

Meanwhile, back east, legislation was making its rounds which, when they were inevitably passed, legalized gay marriage, but also included protections for the Churches so that they could not be targeted, legally or otherwise, for refusal to service gay marriages or recognize them. Interestingly, the LDS Church was silent then... California, however, offered no such protections.

Churches do have a right to be legitimately concerned. After all, we are seeing all kinds of lawsuits against businesses who are run by Christians and refuse to participate in Gay nuptials. Reports of pastors arrested for preaching that homosexuality is a sin are not uncommon in Europe, or even Canada. Sadly, it happens all the time. Understandably, the churches do not want to see legalized persecution against Christianity over this issue, as it has overseas.

This is my hypothesis (as in everything I have to present as supporting evidence is only circumstantial): I think that for many on the right, it's more a fear of seeing their churches forced to perform, facilitate, and recognize marriages that are against their faith. And if you don't think the government would make a church act against its conscious...? The so called "War on

Women?" Yeah that was actually the Obama administration's war on the Catholic Church, trying to force them to offer contraception to their employees as a part of their health care plans, even though it violates key tenants of the Catholic faith. The rest of it was a figment of MSNBC's and CNN's imagination.

So where do we compromise? The right has always held out civil unions as the compromise. We're not unwilling to grant gay couples the same legal benefits of marriage, insurance, tax breaks, etc. That's never been an issue for us. However, for many on the right, the term marriage is exclusive to one man and one woman as a religious tradition, which pre-dates government. Any attempts to change that definition and tradition is an unwarranted and unreasonable attack on our beliefs, our culture and our faith.

I won't pretend that Jefferson would have been okay with gay marriage. By today's standards, he was a Bible thumper... again by *today's* standards. But at the end of the day, the core idea of Jeffersonianism is liberty. Do not force the Churches to perform, acknowledge or redefine these marriages. Don't sue, prosecute or persecute our churches. Accept the compromise of a civil union. You can call the civil ceremony whatever you want, but if it's a government marriage license or document, whether homosexual or heterosexual, then the law should refer to it as a civil unions, and it should only be performed by *willing* civil servants. No one morally opposed to this should be forced to act against their religious principals, not now, not later, not ever. Of course faiths who are not opposed to homosexuality should be able to perform these ceremonies and call it marriage if they are willing to redefine marriage. Then you can call it whatever you want personally, while letting the standard traditional definition of marriage stand in religious communities who would like to maintain their cultural norms. Stated differently, and more simply: Let the religious documents use the term marriage, while the government documents use the term civil union.

This isn't an unreasonable offer. Gays are already equal under the law. They have the same rights to marriage that I do. They are free to marry the opposite sex. What they are advocating is a change to that law that will allow them new privileges. When a guy and a gal marry it's a marriage, in any other arrangement it's not unfair to call it something else. After all a Nintendo and a PlayStation are the same general idea, but they are, in practical and functional terms, different. We don't call a Playstation a Nintendo just because it also plays games, and Sony isn't organizing kiss-ins in Redmond Washington to protest the fact that they can't call their device a Nintendo.

We will respect your right to have legally recognized commitments and the corresponding ceremonies and all the legal perks, if such exist, that go with it. Please just respect our religious traditions and please be careful how much time you're spending staring into the abyss. Don't become the monsters you seek to fight. Peace can be had if both sides are willing to compromise, but remember compromise means giving me something I want and I want the definition of marriage to go untouched by the law, even if a civil union is a similar idea.

You know, ideally the solution would be to get the government out of marriage all together. I don't know why government needs to be involved in this process. The individual religious institutions and the individuals involved should be the only people getting to define this as it is a commitment between two people and God, but that is an idea that gets me called "libertarian" and then chased out with pitchforks and torches. This solution will not pass in any state or federal legislative process. The aforementioned compromise will, and I would be surprised indeed if we couldn't even get it done in Utah. But as with my experience in high school, this discussion will indeed bring out the extremes on both sides. And by extreme, I mean someone who is willing to cause another physical harm for their beliefs, not someone who merely disagrees with the Progressives.

With the recent rulings by SCOTUS, which tossed out key parts of DOMA and hung the religious community out to dry on Prop Eight, compromise on this issue is more important than ever if a solution is to be found which will preserve religious liberty in the process.

1-Props to Obama Did he help push California's gay-marriage ban over the top? By Farhad Manjoo, www.slate.com. http://www.slate.com/articles/news_and_politics/politics/2008/11/props_to_oba ma.html Accessed 1/17/2014

Chapter Nine: BSL is BS

For the uninitiated, BSL is Breed Specific Legislation and it is among the more sinister tyrannies facing our nation. Thanks to the deranged fantasies of the liberal media, the quintessential American Dog, the American Pit-bull Terrier, and its many cousin breeds, has been demonized, and in many cities seized and exterminated without having done anything wrong. All because the municipal governments have identified the following traits as indicative of a dangerous dog: A short nose, a flat, squared head, a medium tail and about the biggest dopey smile you'll ever see. This is Aerith. She is one of two special dogs which changed my life. This picture was taken by my sister in-law, an independent photographer, because she found Aerith unbearably cute. We often joke that

Aerith is so cute you can hardly bare-eth. Isn't she adorable? I ask you, does she look dangerous to you?

Her vet told me she's a purebred American Staffordshire Terrier. The other one I won't include a picture of, and I'll explain why shortly, but she was actually a Rhodesian Ridgeback-Amstaff-Collie mix, mostly Ridgeback and Staffy. We named her Tifa. Don't worry, there is a happy ending, but we only had her a year and half when she got upset with Aerith and snapped at her. Now, all dogs in multi-dog families have incidents like this from time to time, but my family's finances collapsed a few years ago, so we've been renting out my mother's basement. Yeah I know, laugh, get it out of your system, ya done? Okay-My sister's ex-husband is one of those typical know it all twits when it comes to pitt bulls. Naturally, when he heard about Tifa's temper tantrum, he declared the house unsafe for his daughters, my nieces, because there's a Pittbull. To keep the peace we had to give up Tifa.

This unfortunate turn of events broke our hearts. Thankfully, when we explained what happened to the shelter, they confirmed what my wife and I had suspected; Tifa was being a typical female dog who hadn't been spayed yet and was testing the pack pecking order. They fixed her, fell in love with her and very quickly found her a new home, where I understand she is living happily ever after. Sadly, not every shelter is as enlightened as the one we turned Tifa over to. I spent that day bawling my eyes out because I though for sure Tifa would be put down. I was beyond relieved when my wife told me the news when I got off work that day.

I still bawled for days after that happened. What wasn't fair is that my mom's cocker spaniel has actually attacked the other dogs in the household and no one has said boo about it, but introduce a mutt with a tiny bit of Pitt-Bull in her blood and it's a problem. That sort of ignorance makes me sick.

The ignorance of what Pitt Bulls are actually like has led to a lot of tragedy. Although Tifa got a happy ending, and our Aerith is currently living out her happily ever after with us, many pitt bulls' stories don't end on a happy note. Aerith's certainly didn't begin on one. She was found by my boss, abandoned in the canyons, emaciated and covered in bite marks. Now, we can only guess as to how she got that way, but Aerith hung around the area where my boss was and finally got brave enough to ask for food. My boss decided to take her home, but couldn't keep her and so she offered her to me. Aerith latched onto me right away, though she was afraid of everyone but my wife and I.

During our first several months with her, we watched a dog, who very clearly had been horribly abused, adjust to normalcy. Initially, she would only go potty at 7AM and again at 7PM. She would eat at 7:30 AM, and 7:30 PM, but only a mouthful each time. She suffered from terrible nightmares that were awful to watch, so my wife and I began to position her between us at night, and we would just hold her until the nightmares ceased and she would ease into a comfortable calm. Today, she cannot sleep unless it's between us, or on top of my pillows.

We have had her four years now. She is five. In that time, not once has she exhibited any sort of aggressive behavior. In fact, everyone who has taken the time to get to know her *adores* her. They tell me she breaks all stereotypes. She is the girliest dog on the planet. If they made a purse big enough for her, she'd sit in it happily. When my wife does her nails, Aerith insists on having hers done. She loves to have daddy hold her paw like a little girl. She is easily startled by loud noises and hides whenever there's a scary movie on. She steals anything that is soft and pink and loves to be sprinkled with glitter, and also steals my pillow. She has a stuffed toy pig she babies like it was a puppy. You cannot tell me this is a dangerous dog. She is not.

Our Amstaff is an angel. She is a very sedentary dog. The emaciated, bitten and bruised little girl my boss rescued is now a pudgy, happy, healthy dog who not only is not afraid of people, but loves them and is eager to please and eager to make new friends to cuddle with. She dotes on my nieces, cuddles the cat, cleans the cocker spaniel, guards the sugar glider and uses teddy bears as pillows, especially the pink ones.

Aerith is as sweet as her namesake, so if you've named your dog Sephiroth please stay far, far away. Luckily, there are no breed bans that I am aware of where I live. You hear about cities in this state mulling over breed bans. Thankfully, either the city councils or mayors strike them down, not wanting to violate the individual liberty and personal responsibility of the responsible dog owner, but that isn't stopping the Pitt-bull haters from trying.

It's funny that Pitt-bull haters are often the same Progressives who call for compassion for people who break the law to come across the border and say, "we don't want to break up families," when we talk about enforcing immigration laws. Too often, they are perfectly happy to barge into your house unannounced, in the middle of the night, confiscate your dog and kill it even though it has never hurt anyone. Most dog owners would consider that breaking up families. And yet there are no calls for compassion for these families who are literally guilty of no other crime but loving one of God's creatures, just one the Liberal Media has decided it hates. I wonder, is it because it's the all AMERICAN Pitt-Bull Terrier? Would it receive as much hate if it was the English Staffordshire Terrier? Or the African Bully Terrier?

The fact is that dog attacks are very rare and Pit-bull attacks account for only a fraction of those attacks.-1) When viewed without emotionalism and sensationalism, the facts often include either a dog which has suffered abuse, or trying to defend its family, territory or offspring. Everyone needs to see the documentary, *Beyond the Myth*. It is a fantastic and refreshingly honest look at the situation, backed with a slew of research and statistics that will tell you everything that you need to know.

Sensationalism and irresponsible owners are the problem, not the dog. Ask anyone who knows Aerith. t\The dog so loved by our friends and neighbors, she has been nicknamed "the princess." This dog has been through some kind of traumatic event, yet under the care of a loving family she has become a cuddle bug, a nanny and a great comfort. All she ever asks in exchange for all her hard work is the occasional belly rub.

The American Pitt-bull Terrier was originally bred to be stuck in a pit and used as bait for bulls and bears. Thank goodness that practice was deemed inhumane and was banned. At that point, there was a divergence in its use. Some people took it home where it was found that they make loyal nannies and phenomenal working dogs. They excel at hunting varmint and stealing pillows, but there were those who used the dog for fighting, because of the dog's strength not because of its aggression.

Pitts are not a naturally aggressive breed, that aggression has to be trained into them. Sadly, there are a number of people looking to get a dog with a "macho" appearance who have cropped their ears, docked their tails, and encouraged the dog to act "tough". It is because there are people out there who have trained their Pitts to be aggressive in this way that it has a bad rap. If the dog is well socialized and well-loved, it is the most loyal, loving, good-natured pet you will ever own. A very telling photo appears on the web featuring the Little Rascal's Pitt-bull, Petey, and the text, "Nobody was afraid of me back then."

The fact is that this used to be the all American dog, well-loved and adored, but because of dog fighters and the American news media, who hate anything American, the image of this innocent and lovable breed has been changed dramatically. The dogs who are made to fight are often killed by their owners when they lose. You hear stories of dogs being hooked up to jumper cables, hung by their necks, or drowned. God has made a very special place in Hell for Michael Vick, to burn forever for what he did to his dogs. People like Vick should never be allowed to go anywhere near a dog after putting them through that kind of abuse. We make sex offenders enter into a registry, people who brutally beat their dogs to death ought to do likewise. The twisted news media may have forgiven Vick, but I will not. Those pups who do find loving homes are all too often ripped from them and terminated with extreme prejudice, without due cause, by the municipalities who are not content to leave a peaceful and quiet family alone.

I look at my sweet Aerith and all the scars on her body from tooth and claw marks. I remember holding her as she struggled through one nightmare after another, how my scared and emaciated rescue has, in the end, done more to rescue me by opening my heart to the love like nothing else I have ever experienced with any other pet. We have numerous friends who also have APBTs or Amstaffs and their experiences are not dissimilar.

The compromise is this. Leave the dogs alone, or at least treat them as individual cases. If my dog does something wrong, fine but don't round her up in the middle of the night just because of her breed, as was done in Denver, Colorado a few years ago. The situation is so sever one might think it impossible, yet beginning May 9th, 2005, Denver Police literally began raiding peoples home, rounding them up and summarily executing them without due cause. Pictures of mass graves of Pittbulls in Denver have surfaced all over the web. Here is just one of many example. http://cheezburger.com/7498655488. Here is another: http://dogs.knoji.com/breed-specific-legislation/. There are many, many more. You need to see them, because you need to understand this is absolutely real. This unimaginable horror can, and will happen in every municipality that accepts any kind of breed specific legislation.

Rather than focusing all ire on the dogs, we should focus on getting rid of dog fighting instead. This dog thrives in loving homes and returns the love it receives with kisses and cuddles. Taken away from that love, trained to hate and kill in a dog fighting club, will change its behavior. Rather than eliminate the All-American Dog, let's eliminate the cause of its aggression: the Dog Fighting Clubs. They're already illegal, but let's work within our communities to make sure they are eliminated.

On a happier note, it turns out the very original Petey the Pup's ring around his eye was actually mostly real. The makeup artists on the set of Little Rascals only had to close the loop with makeup. Apparently, he made it into *Ripley's Believe it or Not* for his unique markings.

-1) Derived from Corona Research, Dog bites in Colorado, Report of Dog Bite Incidents Reported to Animal Control July 2007-June 2008, Coronoa Research Inc, 2009. Pg 21

Chapter 10: Agenda 21 Twenty-One Years Too Late...

Agenda 21 is something that happened at the UN Conference on Environment and Development in Rio De Janeiro, Brazil in 1992. Designed to combat global warming, this plan calls for limiting human access to resources, limiting where they can live and severely limiting access to energy by taking UN sponsored ideas right to the municipality. Then they force the municipality to pass ideological and restrictive policies, all in the name of supposedly saving the earth. The general concepts and tenants are scary enough that the GOP placed a plank in their platform criticizing it as a threat to national sovereignty and to property rights. I'm actually going to just advise you to go look it up on your own because to explain it is going to take too much time and I don't feel like putting on my tin foil hat right now. Not to disparage those in the thick of the fight against it, but we are twenty-one years too late to really go after this program without sounding like a kook; ergo opposing this authoritarian nightmare will require us to stop fighting the last war of attrition against it and review our tactics.

That said, please do read *Behind the Green* Mask by Rosa Koire, the creator of www.democratsagainstagenda21.com. The basic concerns she writes about can be summarized thusly: The effort by the UN is yet another gimmick to create an inventory and mechanism to redistribute all the world's resources and arguably, assume control of the means of distribution and production. On its surface, it looks like your typical communist dribble. However, its unintended consequences seem like a new form of tyranny where the rationale behind it is this save the world nonsense that drives the eco fascists, as opposed to the crazy altruism at the expense of everyone but the rich liberals in Hollywood crowd. Agenda 21 is whipping up all kinds of activist groups into a frenzy, but the UN has, last time I checked, deleted all references to it from their website so you can't get the goods from the horse's mouth anymore. What's worse is that the news media (always in league with the side of evil) is mocking these activists and doesn't care if the critics of Agenda 21 are Liberal Democrats (as is Rosa Koire) or Libertarians like Glenn Beck.

There are key phrases we should look out for, not just for Agenda 21 but for policy in general. Phrases such as references to carbon emissions, economic fairness or equality, social justice, sustainability must all be met with scrutiny and skepticism. It seems that every time I hear politicians use these phrases, something follows which smacks of Auschwitz. Nevertheless, fighting this one head on will not yield anything other than you and your group being mocked relentlessly by the media. That said, a change of tactics is needed.

Let's refrain from using the key words they mock shall we? Let's not talk of Agenda 21. Had we gone after it in 1992, we'd have more people willing to listen, but twenty-one years out? Not so much. Instead, at your local town hall meetings listen for their key words and then pounce... Politely... with questions about what a policy means for your cost of living, for your freedom, for your family. The opposition to this green tyranny needs a human face and unfortunately the left doesn't count Glenn Beck. This is odd because it seems to me they liked him when he was going after Bush.... It must suck to be consistent, but I digress. Putting a human face on the opposition means doing to the Progressives, who control your city, what they are doing to you. Use emotion as your weapon. Appeal to their sense of decency. Point out how these policies impact your personal life and makes it harder for your family.

In example, recently Tooele County got slapped with a proposal for an 82% tax hike. Some have responded by pointing out that part of Agenda 21 is, allegedly, raising suburban taxes so high it forces people back into the cities. Well, a substantial tax increase of this magnitude is going to hurt your family. Fighting back against this can only be successful if the masses can feel for you. Calling it Agenda 21 will only get the critic dismissed as conspiracy theorist, even though it is real and even though some of its goals are quite sinister, if you put humanity and liberty first as I do. That is why it needs to be attacked as individual policies, using their unintended consequences to your wallet and personal freedom, not the concentration camps Harriet Park and Glenn Beck's fictional novel warn of. Remember critics of the Nazis were called nuts too, look what was done to Sophie Scholl. Ergo we must find a means of addressing our concerns in a manner that the media cannot mock without looking heartless themselves.

I am all for being a good steward to the planet, I consider myself a reasonable environmentalist, but I am unwilling to do anything which compromises liberty.

I don't like pollution, I don't want dirty air, or dirty water, or old women and sick children to fend for themselves as Obama has alleged. But there's only so much that can be taken from me before you start to hurt me, and I am already there. The average American needs their municipalities to be looking at reducing their costs of living, especially since the federal government won't. These are the angles that must be applied to push back against this.

Again, I want you to go research Agenda 21 for yourself. Be aware of it, but don't let the enemy see you fighting against it, or you will have a tin foil hat photo-shopped to you. That is the game they are playing now. It worked against Glenn Beck and the Tea Party and they'll do it to you too. They're Progressives, they don't want to debate the issue (or any issue), so they'll just call you names until you go away. Don't let them name call. Instead, appeal to the heart of those around you.

Each plank of the UN Agenda 21 will have to be picked apart individually. After all, if placed on a municipality's desk in full, the thing would never pass, but in small chunks it can, it might and in some places it has. Ergo, we must remain vigilant, but our eyes must be on the lookout for individual policies, not one big giant conspiracy. Taken bit by bit, it can be taken apart, especially when people are made aware of the individual costs to their wallets and their liberties.

Luckily, there are people on the left and right who are opposed to these programs. I mentioned www.democratsagainstagenda21.com. The right and the left should be able to work together to pull this apart for the simple reason that, as far into tyranny we have sojourned, there is a bridge too far for both of us and when we come to that bridge, we should not be afraid to stand together.

Chapter 11: The Ron Paul Revolution Is Dead

Long, Live the Rand Paul Revolution

In the interest of full disclosure, I have supported Ron Paul in the past, but have always supported the party's nominee because it's good politics. I've adhered strictly to Ronald Reagan's 11th commandment of not speaking ill of fellow Republicans. I am doing so here, but only in the hopes of making things better for our party, and more importantly the grass roots who I favor over the establishment. Still, the establishment is right about some things, especially on political mechanics. They're better at word-smithing than the grass roots most of the time. They can be, however, less interested in the party platform and adherence to it. I'll write about that later, but here I want to focus on Libertarians, specifically what the Utah GOP disparagingly refers to as "Ron Paulers," or "Paulbots."

Ron Paul is right on domestic issues and in general on foreign policy. Call me an isolationist if you want, but the reality is that our military is spread too thin, our enemy ill-defined and our moral high ground lost. Dr. Paul's stance on Israel isn't one of hostility, but neutrality. Dr. Paul is all about a return to the Monroe Doctrine of noninterventionism, and although I stand with Israel and pray for them, I mostly agree with Dr Paul on this too.

However, I have been in trouble with the Paulbots on a few occasions myself, and I know what it's like to be the recipient of their ire. Ron Paul once proposed on his You Tube page that the States can secede if they wanted to. I replied saying that route is dangerous because it would lead to a second civil war. I proposed that if we are that dissatisfied with things, we ought to consider a Constitutional Convention as an alternative. This video is the only one I did to exceed 400 views, reaching well over 1,000 and the response was nasty. I deleted the worst and most vile comments, but was shocked at the behavior of fellow Ron Paul supporters. I was civil in my presentation as was Dr Paul, but not my fellow Ron Paul supporters.

I liked a lot of what Ron Paul had to say over all. However, he lost the primary. When that happened, I switched over to the Romney camp. Even though it was clear there was no path to victory for Paul, his other supporters tool to calling me "neo-con," "traitor," and a "Progressive." Really? Now I know what Jefferson had to deal with when he decided to back James Madison over James Monroe! Sheesh! I didn't abandon my values. Ron Paul wasn't going to be on the ticket. All I did was follow the Buckley rule: I supported the most conservative candidate who can win. While Mitt Romney was a self-described Moderate, he was much closer to me than Obama. While his values were not lock and step with mine, he ran a remarkable campaign as an adult, whereas Obama was running like a twelve-year-old boy. Romney, a numbers guy like myself, could be reasoned with. In contrast, Obama considers anything that is not one hundred percent of what he wants a refusal to compromise.

Now we're facing losing the second amendment. Obamacare will never be repealed, and the Federal Reserve Bank will never be audited. Everything Ron Paul was fighting for has been lost and the establishment is likely to try and find someone even less conservative for 2016; likely Chris Christi.

Ron Paulers share some responsibility for the 2012 election results because they either got behind Libertarian dunce and third party candidate, Gary Johnson, or stayed home. We only needed 2.8 million more votes to oust the Dictator-In-Chief who can't wait for Congress. I know it was the Libertarians had a role to play, because it was they who were boasting about it on Facebook and calling radio shows to brag that they stayed home. We have a very short amount of time ahead of us in which we can turn things around, and get our country back on track, or slow things down enough to give us more time to prevent total economic collapse. I happen to agree that a surface glimpse of Romney's record left much to be desired. So too did Reagan's track record as governor of California. For that matter, Calvin Coolidge had signed on to the Progressive movement before jumping off that band wagon later in his career. That said, the profound transformation of Calvin Coolidge and Ronald Reagan should be an historical precedence that just because someone did dumb things earlier in their career, does not mean they will be bad presidents. That historical precedence was not enough to convince some Libertarians, though it is enough for Jeffersonian Republicans like myself.

Enter Gary Johnson. In years past, when I thought there was a third party candidate who was clearly the better option and I knew the Democrat would lose, I would enter my protest vote. I did not vote for Bush in '04. In a race this close, I couldn't justify doing that again, especially since it was so clear (I must apologize for my upcoming harshness) that Gary Johnson was not the better candidate that anyone with half a brain cell, anyone with any semblance of intelligence, should have been able to see this.

I had seen Gary Johnson on TV. I saw him in the debate he participated in. He's been on Stossel and other Fox News shows. Each and every time I saw him, he came off as an inarticulate moron. His answers to each question always bore a remarkable resemblance to, "I have a cunning plan!" followed by nothing of substance. The Libertarian Party was essentially running S. Baldrick for president. How this guy has managed to get as far in his life as he is an enigma to me. I suppose plenty of stupid people manage to finagle their way into positions of influence. Paul Krugmen has managed to convince the New York Times to take him seriously, even though he thinks that the best way to help the economy is to stage a space alien invasion.-1.

Gary Johnson's idiocracy is well documented, but comes in a different form. This man is no John Galt. Unlike John Galt, who can go on for 60 pages about the problems of America and keep you engaged, Gary Johnson cannot articulate much of anything. Libertarians and their anarchist comrades have got to win the intellectual argument before an election can be won. They/we have failed to do that. In fact, the extreme behavior of many of the Ron Paulers has turned a lot of people off. I won't name names here (Jake Shannon, Alex Jones) but when I got involved with Utah's GOP in 2010, they were ecstatic to have the libertarians "coming home." Now they can't wait to get rid of them. Instead of trying to have an intelligent conversation, they yelled, they screamed, they called names. They even threatened elected officials, many who were good solid folks who would have been friendly to the cause, had the Libertarians come to the table with a pen, paper and ideas. Instead, they showed up with pitchforks and torches. Now, there is not much of a seat at the Republican table. Rather than admit the egregious error in behavior, now many Libertarians are vowing to destroy the GOP, even though that efforts ended in Obama being re-elected and the country facing total collapse under his abysmal leadership. I also no longer label myself as a Libertarian. Don't worry, I haven't sold out to the establishment either. I'm going after them next, so if you're a Ron Pauler already upset with me and can't take the critiques, skip on ahead to the next chapter and you'll cheer me on again. But if you'd like the ordinary fat guy's advice on how to fix your movement, keep reading.

What frightened me is that some Libertarians celebrated the fact that pulled votes away from Romney. The impact of Johnson isn't immediate when you look at the electoral "landslide." However, when you consider the fact that most states were decided by a few hundred thousand votes, one or two points, those Libertarian votes could have made the difference. They may have even saved some seats Like Allen Wests and a few other good ones who lost their seats this year.

Some are celebrating, saying that when the country collapses we'll just rebuild it anew. Let's assume Obama is the dictator many fear he is. Is there a history of dictators allowing for opposition parties in the aftermath of their take over? Historically, the Libertarian Party mounted quite a resistance to Hitler's Nazi party, and what a great job they did keeping people from starving to death in Communist China... oh wait... The opposition parties were all killed... hmm... No, that doesn't end well. There was no Libertarian force to rebuild after those countries collapsed and they collapsed even deeper into tyranny.

If there is real concern that Obama is leading us down the road of a dictatorship and that this country will subsequently collapse, there is no historic examples of a new liberty society emerging from the ashes of such catastrophic failure. The despotic and debauched Weimar Republic collapsed into Nazism, which collapsed into socialism, a smiley-faced version of the latter. Despotism becomes fanaticism, becomes socialism, becomes communism, which is fanaticism. Do you see freedom anywhere in this formula?

The American Revolution was a fluke, a freak of nature. To have a liberty society is so rare on this earth that we should be fighting tooth and nail to preserve it. The best way to do that is not to ensure the second term of a man who, if he continues down this road (bypassing congress and just doing whatever he wants by executive order, and spending us off a cliff) will inevitably lead us toward despotism. If not at his own hands, by setting the stage for a future despot.

Even if Romney only slowed things down, it would have bought us more time to win the intellectual debate, which must be won to turn this ship around. The selection of Paul Ryan, to me, symbolizes Romney's willingness to have those conversations. If the Libertarians could put down their clubs for a moment and look at the good Ryan has done in congress, they would find that while Ryan's voting record is imperfect, he has been one of a very few who has been talking of spending cuts and entitlement reform. He has even been exploring privatization of some programs, even though such notions have been demagogued in the media for generations. Paul Ryan has been trying to urge people to have this adult conversation for 14 years. Does he go far enough? No! But he's a good start!

With the election of Mitt Romney, the opportunity existed for Libertarians to engage in the national conversation about the direction this country once more. Romney may have been on the wrong side of many issues in the past, but his selection of Ryan shows he was serious about having that discussion. Since Obama was re-elected, at best, we can count on four more years of, "the reason that we have this problem is because there's Republicans." This will evolve into, "if there weren't Republicans we wouldn't have this problem. What? What's that you say? Round up the Republicans and throw them in ovens? Now there's a great idea! We can't wait for Congress! I'll just do it by executive order and while we're at it, let's toss in those irritating radical extreme Tea Baggers, Jews and Libertarians too... or blow them up with unmanned drones! Oh this will be so much fun!" Don't doubt me. You will not have a seat at the table since Obama was re-elected and the GOP will now turn their spears on you to help suppress your voice in the name of preventing any further embarrassments.

In all fairness, much of this insanity isn't Ron Paul's fault. His son Rand is getting along well with both the Libertarian and Establishment wing of the GOP, except Lindsay Graham, Chris Christie and John McCain, but they've never liked anyone in their own party. He gets along fine with Mitch McConnell and others. However, Ron's supporters tend to be fans of a man who is either a left over from the annoying John Birch Society, or a Left Wing cointellpro operator, Alex Jones. Jones' antics are so fake and over the top though that I tend to believe he is the latter, a more crude and primitive version of Stephen Colbert. But, just as Mike Huckabee seemed oblivious to the fact that Colbert is mocking us, so to do fans of Alex Jones. I mean why else would the guy talk about the Bilderberg Meetings the way he does? The Bilderberg Meetings are secretive meetings where the world's elite get together and talk about God only knows what... literally... So naturally, some people are suspicious of them. While that suspicion is normal (we all fear what we don't understand) Alex Jones has to toss in baseless allegations that the group is eating barbequed babies wrapped in gold tin foil. Impossible, no one could commit such a horrible crime as infanticide and cannibalism without someone catching it on a phone camera and putting it online.

Jones is the reality of what Glenn Beck has been accused of. Most of what people say about Beck was actually done by Jones. Beck may have an unconventional approach to the news, but at least he usually backs himself up with verifiable facts. Jones makes crazy accusations and offers no proof whatsoever. It was Jones, not Beck, who put forward the FEMA camp conspiracy theory. Beck lampooned it. In fact, Jones abhors Beck, believing him to be part of the "conspiracy." Beck's lampooning of the issue got him accused of promoting the conspiracy theory by the left, but the reality is this is Alex Jones' work, not Beck's.

I bring this up because unseasoned activists don't have professional training on how to behave in politics. Thus they just did to Obama what they saw people on the left, and Alex Jones, do to George W. Bush. The left can complain that the way that Obama is being treated is unprecedented, but at least he has a very liberal media coddling him. Bush didn't. In addition to the media promoting protesters like Code Pink, the media also promoted the 9-11 Truther movement lead by Alex Jones, whose behavior isn't much different from the left wing protesters the media would whip into a frenzy against Bush. Ergo, these young Libertarians haven't exactly had good role models and thus have alienated many who would otherwise be friends.

I, however, benefit from growing up with John Stossel being one of my parent's favorites, as well as Milton Friedman. My dad used to watch these two gentlemen on TV, so I learned about Free Markets from them. They never antagonized their opposition. Instead, they used logic and reason to make their case. Then I met Dr. Glenn J. Kimber of the Thomas Jefferson Center for Constitutional Restoration. On one occasion, early on, after I had posted a video on You Tube calling Obama a communist, Dr. Kimber pulled me off to the side after class and told me, "when you go out and try to teach people don't be obnoxious. Funny is fine, but try to understand that if you were taught what Obama has been taught, you would believe what he believes and you would do what he is doing." I never asked if that was his response to my video or what brought that comment on but I held that message to heart.

Then I had a chat with Utah Governor Herbert once, he first urged me to urge my Libertarian friends to read the party platform. He was convinced they would like it. Then he urged me to keep my conservative values at heart, but to use a moderate tone. I have a great respect for both men and I don't presume to know what brought on this advice, but because both are men I admire, I have tried hard to conduct myself in a manner where logic and reason would prevail over crass emotionalism. It's hard, but Stossel and Friedman are the models that Libertarians ought to be looking for. Sadly, most were brought into the fold as part of the 9-11 Truther movement.

Such hostility toward fellow right wingers has caused me to distance myself from the Libertarians at large. I love these guys. They're good people. Most would lump me in with them ideologically and I don't mind being called Libertarian, where as I will get mad if people call me Conservative. I am, however, fortunate in that my role model wasn't Alex Jones. He has encouraged the damaging philosophy that if you do not agree with the Libertarians 100% of the time, then you are the enemy. Too many Libertarian activists have adopted this idea.

This behavior is part of the reason that the John Birch Society fell apart. Those who didn't agree with them 100% of the time were made enemies of the movement, forcing the LDS Church to put out a statement distancing themselves from it. William Buckley, who had previously been their ally, would also later urge the GOP to eschew them. This, despite the fact that both the LDS Church and Buckley had been historically very anti-Communist.

Libertarians must not allow themselves to fall into the trap of exlusion, or they will be rendered as ineffective as Alex Jones. Look at how popular Stossel is as opposed to even Judge Andrew Napolitano, who I like, but is certainly a lot more boisterous than his Fox colleague. Stossel's show is going strong, while Napolitano has been reduced to a Fox News Contributor for his show, Freedom Watch, failing to maintain an audience. Libertarians must adopt Reagan's philosophy of "no enemies on the right."

Libertarian ideology is highly intellectual, and therefore logic and reason should be a central tenant to it. We ought to conduct ourselves in politics as a Vulcan would... and no I'm not being humorous. However logic and reason eschew conspiracy theories and only focus on real irrefutable facts. Logic and reason also doesn't yell and scream at people who ought to be natural allies. Logic and reason don't engage in behind the scenes shenanigans to try and deny a Republican candidate votes he rightfully won in a State Primary.

Of the many egregious errors the Libertarians made in the last election cycle, the worst was to try to use loopholes in the election rules to get their delegates elected to represent their state's vote in Nevada, where Romney won the Primary. Based on the final tallies, Ron Paul legitimately won Maine, but definitely not Nevada where Ron Paul only had eight delegates and Romney won 20. Nevertheless, Paul supporters won the State's delegate seats and the party leadership and all of those delegate points were handed over to Ron Paul against the Nevada voter's stated intent. Romney won the Primary, but that didn't matter to the Libertarian wing of the party. Similar shenanigans were attempted in other states as well, forcing the GOP establishment to respond.

The establishment went too far as well, refusing to seat rightfully elected delegates known to be sympathetic to Ron Paul, including those who had expressed that they would represent the results of their state election and not pull any shenanigans. Then they had a last second change of the rules rammed through, which allowed the establishment to appoint their own delegates to replace those elected by their respective state. This draconian overreach only exacerbated an already bad situation and the end result was that the Ron Paul supporters had to be escorted out of the convention halls. Of course, they played the victim. They couldn't see that, although they were right that the establishment went too far, so did they. Their chicanery didn't win them any friends in the process, nor accolades from the public at large.

Then, after the election, when American hero Chris Kyle was murdered, Ron Paul put the final nail in the coffin of his own movement when he tweeted, "Chris Kyle's death seems to confirm that 'he who lives by the sword dies by the sword.' Treating PTSD at a firing range doesn't make sense."-2 The heartless and careless thought sparked enough outrage that Paul felt the need to clarify by stating; "As a veteran, I certainly recognize that this weekend's violence and killing of Chris Kyle were a tragic and sad event. My condolences and prayers go out to Mr. Kyle's family. Unconstitutional and unnecessary wars have endless unintended consequences. A policy of non-violence, as Christ preached, would have prevented this and similar tragedies. -REP"-4. The Ron Paulers quickly latched onto this and crafted the feeble defense that Ron Paul didn't mean that Chris Kyle got what he deserved, only that he fulfilled scripture. Hmmm... Let's take a look at the scripture shall we. Open up to Revelations 13: 10

He that leadeth into captivity shall go into captivity: he that [a]killeth with the sword must be killed with the sword. Here is the [b]patience and the faith of the [c]saints.

Most people would interpret this as a warning and a rebuke of violence saying, basically, if you live a violent life style and get killed, you got your comeuppance. There's no need to re-interpret scripture to avoid the reality that Ron Paul said Chris Kyle got what he deserved. It was a cruel and insensitive statement. It's one thing to be anti-war. So am I! It's quite another to make snarky remarks about a fallen American Hero who put on the uniform, so that Ron Paul would continue to have the right to make snarky remarks about people who put on the uniform.

The Ron Paul Revolution is dead and they have no one to blame but themselves. The tragedy is only made worse by their inability to focus on issues that really matter to people. Most people don't care about legalizing pot. Now isn't the time to push for that when people are worried about jobs, or how to pay off the Government's debt, or how to find a wage large enough to get off welfare... Yet leave it to Libertarians to get distracted with the "squirrel!" issues of pot, prostitution and other divisive and anarchistic ideas.

Thankfully Rand Paul's approach has been much more palatable. He's a Libertarian-Republican, like his father, but he's been far less hostile to people who aren't lock-in-step with him, though the media is treating him like he were crazy. He has engaged in a much more civil dialogue that I believe could re-ignite the flame of the liberty movement. This assumes his supporters will use logic and reason as their approach to policy going forward, rather than shrill name calling, and cheap political tricks. Rand Paul's recent filibuster shows a willingness to tackle tough issues head on, though if you actually watched him, he was cordial and polite during the entire process. He wasn't waving the red shirt as we say, though John McCain and Lindsay Graham sure did later on in response but again, those two have never liked the people in their own party.

If the Liberty movement is to be revived, it must be through civil discourse and quiet dignity. George Washington was not profane, nor was he subject to fits of rage. Washington built alliances and so must we. Reagan built alliances, so must we. Libertarians and Republicans often have but a hair's breadth of difference between them on general principals. There is plenty of room for friendly relationships. It's just that Libertarians tend to be rude and easily distracted, as mentioned previously, by less important issues. If they stay focused on economic liberty and sound money, or even auditing the fed (which 100% of the GOP is behind now), by moderating their tone and behavior, and by choosing their battles more wisely, they could make an explosive comeback in 2014. However, they will only be welcomed by the public at large if they can play   nice.

References:

-1 To see this insanity the quickest way to an un-scrubbed copy is here: http://www.youtube.com/watch?v=S8TKfq10v3o at about 2:45 in

-2 Ron Paul clarifies comments on death of Navy SEAL sniper- Published 2-6-13 Read more: http://www.foxnews.com/politics/2013/02/06/ron-paul-clarifies-comments-on-death-navy-seal-member/#ixzz2L5Ejm8Es Accessed 2-16-13

-3 Ibid

Chapter 12: Everything In Moderation Without Defining "Moderate"

The ultimate question I would like to ask everyone is, "what the devil is a 'moderate'?" I ask this because I used to consider myself a moderate, or constitutional centrist, but now people tell me I'm extreme (which is not only rude but also annoying.) Real extremism (i.e. Occupy Wall Street) is an anathema to me. While learning about the Constitution at the Thomas Jefferson Center for Constitutional Restoration, I learned a very clear definition for left wing extremism, right wing extremism and moderate. Below is a recreation of the *only* political paradigm chart I know of that is easy to understand. Remove all the nuance and this is all you need.

Example 1.

Tyranny	Constitution/Moderate	Anarchy
	M	
	E	

So to me, a moderate is someone who is fighting for a return to the simplicity of the constitutionally limited government our founders set up. If you're a right wing extremists, then you are fighting for anarchy. If you are a left wing extremists, then you are fighting for tyranny, or authoritarianism. In other words, a swastika, or hammer and sickle on a red flag is extreme. A black flag is extreme… but a Gadston flag? Not so much. In fact the Gadston Flag folks are just trying to preserve the America they grew up in. How is that extreme? Well it's extreme if you understand where the Progressives in both parties have dragged our government in the last 100 years.

Example 2.

Tyranny			Constitution/Moderate	Anarchy
	D e m s	R e p s	**M** **E**	

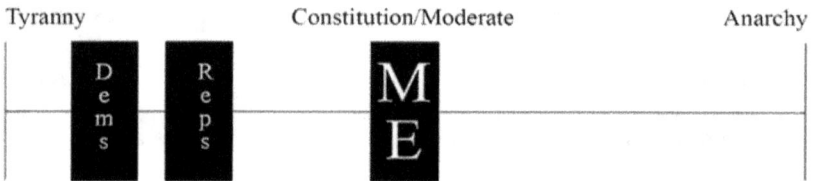

See a problem here? I haven't moved but they have. Everything looks extreme from so far to the left. Make no mistake, the more programs they put in place, the more they regulate, the more paperwork you have to fill out, the more they involve themselves in your personal affairs (i.e. healthcare), the more of your money they take the less free you are. It is not moderate to refuse to stand against these programs. It is not moderate to refuse to repeal, or at least defund, Obamacare. There is nothing moderate about Obamacare, or Obama. Both are a product of the extreme left.

We have so many new regulations added every year, hundreds of thousands of new pages… *every year*. There's a good chance you are breaking laws, and don't even know it, just living your ordinary day to day life. We have a 75,000 page tax code that no one understands. We have now a government healthcare system that will allow for a panel of unelected bureaucrats to make life or death decision for you. The proposed cap and trade policies would threaten to limit your use of energy. How much you watch TV, play on the Internet, have your porch light on would all be affected by these government proposals. President Obama was completely honest that the intent would be to cause energy prices to, in his own words "necessarily skyrocket."-1

Gas taxes drive up the cost of travel. Food taxes drive up the price of putting dinner on your table. Sin taxes... property taxes... it all impacts your behavior. Now, the aforementioned which are voluntary transactions, I am okay with. However, some are deliberately crafted to impact your behavior and thus exercise control. Is it extreme to suggest that the people ought to shape their government and not the inverse? Should the government have a say in what you watch, what you eat, where you work, or how much or how little you are paid? Perhaps you should be making those decisions.

Is a man even entitled at all to the fruits of his labors? Americans are looking for leaders who are prepared to answer that question. Can the "moderate" establishment answer it? If the answer is no, what exactly was the sin of the Democratic Party during the Nineteenth Century? The conservative Republicans would say that it was the Democrats claiming the assumption of the power to compel African-Americans to work, not for their own self-interest, but for the benefit of the plantation elites. The Democrats would respond by calling the Republicans extremists… then attacking Fort Sumpter.

What's it like today? Democrats assume the power to compel all Americans to work for the government plantation elites and call those who wish to work for their own self-interest selfish. Republicans want, as Coolidge said, "the American people to work less for the government and more for themselves." Democrats call Republicans extremists…

Before the advent of the Tea Party, Nancy Pelosi, Harry Reid and Barack Obama all used the term "extremists" against the House minority party. At the time the GOP was overwhelmed by a super majority of Democrats in the House and the Senate. They were never a part of any conversations at all, yet their "extremism" was blamed for delays in the stimulus, omnibus and even Obamacare, even though the GOP had no power to push back against any of it. Whatever fighting was going on in Washington was between Democrats.

Before that the Bush era Republicans were deemed "Neo-Radical Conservatives," and the Democrats plastered "Bush-Hitler" posters everywhere and protested the GOP with a level of viciousness Obama has never been subjected to. They treated Bush like garbage, yet decry today the simplest of disagreement in policy with Obama as unprecedented and therefore racist.

Before that, Ronald Reagan was called nuts, stupid and extreme. This game has been going on quite a while, but what shocked me in 2012 is that instead of dismissing these antics as typical left wing nuttiness, the GOP establishment sided with them against their own base voters and grass roots activists.

I don't always agree with Conservatives, nor do I consider myself a Tea Partier, I am a party of one, so far as I know. But the agenda of fiscal responsibility and liberty is one I feel is of the utmost importance and addressing these issues must be done with urgency. Yet, rather than leap onto the bandwagon the GOP establishment cannibalized it.

2012 was a strange year politically. I am still confused by how the GOP's strategy made any sense. Here is the Moderate establishment's road map to victory.

-Join the Democrats in decrying Conservatives as "extremists."

-Where applicable, use scare tactics to whip up the uninformed voter to turn out to caucuses more afraid of their own party than Barack Obama. Have them vote out anyone associated with the so called "extremists."

-Move on from conventions complaining about our own "extreme" candidates, even after most conservatives are wiped out.

-Work against your pick (Todd Akin). Associate them with the Tea Party "extremists" when they say something stupid, even though you helped them to beat two (better) Tea Party candidates in the primaries.

-Run a Moderate presidential candidate who is afraid to criticize Barack Obama.

-Refuse to defend this good and decent man from ludicrous attacks from the left. (IE: He avoided taxes, killed a former employee's wife, hates dogs, is a felon etc.)

-Be surprised when you lose the election, even though you basically told everyone your party was hijacked by extremists. Why exactly would they vote for your party?

-Miss the memo that three million fewer registered Republicans turned out to vote for Romney than what voted for McCain in 2008.

-Miss the point that all this screaming about extremists caused said voters to just sit this one out.

-Proceed to blame said voters for scaring off voters who always vote Democrat anyway (Hispanics), and even if you reached peak support from said demographics (around 40%), it would not have shifted the election... However the missing 3 million Conservatives and Libertarians would have.

-Fail to recognize that if you had turned out your base you'd have won. As Byron York recently pointed out, it would have taken us getting 73% of the Hispanic vote going Republican to make up the lost 3 million conservatives. Obama got 71% of the Hispanic vote-2

-Fail to recognize that converting so large a chunk of a Democratic block is much harder than just being more appealing to your own disenfranchised base.

Minus the emotion this is exactly what the 2012 and the Autopsy Report from Reince Priebus looked like. The Moderate Establishment beat the Conservatives in the party and lost the election in the process. Congratulations. How in the world do you expect to win an election by telling the world your candidates and base are "extremists"? How does it make sense to position yourself for 2014 by saying "you know, the democrats are right about immigration, taxes, spending…" ad nauseam?

In my blog, The Unapologetic Apologist, I have warned repeatedly that only a united Right could stop Obama, the media and the Democrats. I repeat my warning herein; if the Moderate Establishment continues to cannibalize its own base and attack its own candidates you will only succeed in convincing voters who would turn out for you to stay home. Republican Moderates were a crucial tool in the Democrat's war chest. Why?

There is something to be said for the ugly way the Tea Party targeted some of the more established candidates with reckless abandon. But extreme? Hardly. They also did win more than a handful of elections, far more than they've lost, they've earned their stripes, yet only their losses are ever focused on. Sharon

Angle, Christine O'Donnel, Richard Murdoch... but nothing is said of the many establishment picks who have lost. I like Karl Rove, but virtually everyone he backed in 2012 lost. Strangely, that is a point that seems to get lost when discussing whether conservative candidates do better than moderate ones.

Even now, the newspapers decry imaginary right wing extremists while the party falls apart. The richest One Percent of Utah's GOP has banded together to not only destroy the Tea Party, but also Utah's innovative Caucus system. This is the only system, in any state, which grants the ordinary citizen real power to have a say in who the candidates are (I'll explain later.) They argue that extremists took over the party and therefore it needs be destroyed. They list former Utah Governor Olene Walker and former Senator Bob Bennett as victims of these extremists.

It's true that Olene Walker had high approvals, but she wasn't Governor for long before the elections came around and the Democrats announced that they were going to put Scott Matheson, Jr up against her. The son of the famous and well-loved Democratic Governor, Scott Matheson Sr., Matheson the Younger was well positioned to beat a Republican Governor with very little name recognition, so the party *establishment and the delegate*s decided a Republican with a better known name was needed to defend their hold on the governorship. Enter that "right wing extremists," John Huntsman Jr, who himself is hostile toward the Conservative Grass Roots. Huntsman is the poster boy for the Progressive wing of the party, so anyone claiming Olene Walker was ousted by a right wing extremist is nuts.

Bob Bennett wasn't as popular in 2010 as some suggest. In 2010, the Tea Party made up only one of many factions who made up the delegation that was angry about Bennett's spending record and failure to stand up to the left on a myriad of issues. I'd venture a guess that only about 25% of the delegates were formal Tea Party affiliates. I never saw the movement take off in Utah the way it did in other states. While other states would have Tea Party rallies in which thousands of people would show up, here we had tens of people, maybe a couple hundred at best.

The ousting of Bob Bennett was the result of several factions examining his voting record and identifying him as too close to Bush, whom the GOP establishment and Tea Party activists wanted to distance themselves from. After all, aren't all the problems we're facing now Bush's fault? If so, why wouldn't you replace the people who supported Bush's policies lock, stock and barrel? At the time, Bennett was so wildly unpopular for his failings to adhere to conservative principals, and the party platform, that he didn't even clear the second round of voting, netting only 27% of the delegate support.

He was hardly beaten by an extremist though. This is a myth that is circulating. The truth is that moderate, Tim Bridgewater, was the candidate that came the closest to the magic 60% that is needed to clear convention, but he just barely fell short. Mike Lee, our current (and awesome) senator, won the Primary which occurred later. Bridgewater is a great guy and my wife supported him. I endorsed Lee, funny story. Ultimately, these facts do not support the narrative that the Utah GOP was taken over by extremists. Bennett's record was unsatisfactory, and so close to the 2006 and 2008 crash and burn of the GOP, *everyone* was trying to get as far away from Bush as possible and Bennett was seen as a lapdog to the Bush administration.

And for all the moderates who liken the Tea Party to the defunct John Birch Society (they aren't the same), you often forget that the same man who called for distance between the GOP and the JBS is the same man who said George W. Bush is *not* a Conservative-3, and William F. Buckley's comments about Bush had an impact on the party that was very far reaching. I know we have short attention spans in politics, but this is what was actually happening in 2010.

Today Bennett is treated as a fallen hero who sacrificed himself to save us from extremists and was crucified for our sins, after bleeding in the Garden of Gethsemane. In 2012, at Convention he was given an award of appreciation and a standing ovation by a crowd and a party that had forgotten his record. Moreover, they forgot that he actually ran a campaign "Republicans for Granato," against the Republican candidate, Mike Lee, in 2010, and in 2012 he endorsed few Republicans, but many Democrats. It wasn't hard to find billboards in 2012 of Bennett standing with the Democrats, they were everywhere. He has put his thumb of the eye of conservatism every chance he has had, and for a world that is angry about the power of lobbyists in Washington, it seems lost on them that Bennett is now registered as a lobbyist!

Usually, the Party candidate that loses goes on to support the Party candidate who wins, that's what I do. That's what we are almost universally expected to do but when Bennett doesn't do it, or when Chris Christi bear hugs Obama, or Charlie Christ announces that he is now a Democrat, rather than backing their own party, it only validates the concerns of the grass roots activists who deposed them (Chris Christi the non-deposed exception.). Bennett remains a registered Republican, but it would surprise no one who is paying attention in Utah politics if he followed in Charlie Christ's footsteps. He may as well, he's endorsing Democrats left and right anyway. In doing so is doing considerable damage to the party, just like he was before he was deposed with how he was voting.

It's time for the moderate establishment to cut the crap. Grass roots activists are only asking for candidates that will adhere to the party platform. As the old marketing axiom says, "give the people what they want." Republican voters want different things from what Democrat voters want. If the platform is a decree of universally accepted principals for our party then why not adhere to it? Moreover, what exactly is a moderate anyway? I asked the question at the beginning of the chapter, but no one in the party or the local papers has bothered to define it, or "extreme" for that matter. If Moderate means Progressive, get out. You already have one party: the Democrats, as Charlie Christ and rumor has it John Huntsman Jr., have discovered. If by Moderate, you mean you are fiscally conservative but socially liberal and you mean it, then we agree on most issues and we can be friends. Most Tea Partiers would also be your friend because fiscal issues were their primary focus.

Even I have supported good moderates: Utah's Governor, Gary Herbert in 2010, and again in 2012 after convention. A friend of mine was running against him, so I supported him over Gary Herbert because I put friends before politics in all things. Otherwise, I'd have supported Herbert for re-election from the beginning of the 2012 cycle. I think the world of Lt Gov. Bell. West Valley Mayor Mike Winder, is awesome and I endorsed him over conservative Mark Crockett for Salt Lake County Mayor. I supported Tea Partier, Mike Lee, in 2010 and Libertarian-Republican, Morgan Philpot, in the same year. I supported Libertarian-Republican, Carl Wimmer, in 2012, but when he lost at Convention I got behind Conservative, Mia Love, with zeal. I back the person I feel is right for the job, or my own version of the Buckley rule: the candidate who is most like me who can win. Sometimes that's a moderate, sometimes that's a Tea Partier, but it's always a Republican.

I reserve my right to criticize all the factions since I have supported all when they were right, and spoken out against all when they've been wrong. I have never broken Reagan's eleventh commandment of "thou shalt not speak ill of a fellow Republican," until after an election and then only seldom. I want to be clear, I am angry with all the factions, but I feel the Moderate establishment did the most damage by attacking its own base and its own candidates. You never see Tea Partiers on TV agreeing with everything that Piers Morgan is saying about the party, but you do see Jeb Bush on national TV alleging that extremists have taken over the party and would never elect his father or Reagan... Well that's true of anyone with the last name of Bush but are you going to say

William F. Buckley was an extremist because he didn't think Bush was Conservative enough either?

As far as Reagan goes, I am literally a product of the Reagan era. The Tea Party is as well. We're not stupid. We know he had to compromise because the Democrats had congress. We also know that Reagan shifted the paradigm and taxes were lowered over all. We know spending increased, but we recognize that this was due to trying to goad the Communists into a military ramp up we knew they couldn't afford. Thankfully, Reagan's gamble would eventually pay off. We know Reagan closed tax loopholes, but we were never opposed to that. We know that Reagan granted amnesty, but we have to acknowledge that we lost Hispanic support in the next election. As I understand it, Reagan later expressed regret for that, since the Democrats failed to keep their promise to secure the border.

We would love to have Reagan back. To suggest otherwise is insulting. In the 2012 cycle, it was not to find moderate Republicans who were willing to join the liberal hosts of the show they were visiting in demonizing our candidates and the base. It was nearly impossible to find Republicans standing up for Republicans in the media. You cannot win an election employing a strategy like this. The damage from this behavior may be nearly impossible to repair in time for 2014..

We can fix it though, it does mean abandoning the incumbent protection programs. People like Jeb Bush, Charlie Christ, John Huntsman Jr and Bob

Bennett are not good team players and deserve to be deposed. There will be others who will face the wrath of the base grass roots voters. If the party is to be unified, it is best to help them to pick solid candidates who can win, rather than protect the incumbent at all cost. That is assuming they will come back... you better hope they do. You see, in reality the Moderates are about 25% of the party, with Conservatives making up another 25%. Libertarians can add 5-10% more to our base. Add that up you have 55-60% a voting majority. We cannot do this without all of us working together. A failure to unite will only result in further electoral losses. If, however, you think I'm letting the Tea Party off the hook, wait...

...They're next.

-1 Video clip re-posted from original video from the San Francisco Chronicle http://youtu.be/HlTxGHn4sH4 accessed 2-19-13

-2 Winning Hispanic Vote Won't Be Enough for GOP, Byron York 5-6-2013, Townhall.com accessed 6-3-13

-3 Buckley: "Bush not a true conservative." By Amy Clark, CBS News http://www.cbsnews.com/8301-18563_162-1826838.html accessed 2-19-13

-

Chapter 13: Tea Time, Would You Like Some Crumpets?

I am more disappointed with the Tea Party than angry. You guys let me down big time. When I was a precinct chair in Murray, trying to organize my area Neighborhood Caucus Meeting, I ran into more than a few angry Tea Partiers who threatened to oust me because I was an incumbent and therefore evil. I wasn't happy about the Tea Party at first, but the folks who showed up to the caucus ended up being more than reasonable. We talked together, and when the night was over, I was re-elected by acclamation. I then went on to become a Legislative District Chair and had both establishment and tea party friends. Sadly, after the 2010 cycle finances forced me to leave Murray and I had to resign my position.

Murray, Utah has always been held by Democrats, but working together, we ended up just some 200 votes shy of flipping the district for the first time in history, for both the State Senate Seat and State House seat. Something no one thought possible. Imagine what Murray could have been had everyone continued to work together. Indeed, that is the sorry state of the party nationwide. We didn't continue to work together.

After the 2010 cycle, before I moved, we began trying to organize monthly meetings. We were only getting people together every couple of months or so, but I would listen to both Tea Party and non-Tea Party activists intently. Then, I relayed their concerns to the party leaders who would listen, some would even occasionally come out to our meetings.

The meetings only had about ten regular attendees, but the feeling that we were building something was there... or so I thought. Had our group been able to finish what we began in 2010, I imagine 2012 could have looked very different for Murray than it did. Sadly, through a combination of move outs and redistricting, our little team was split apart. That wasn't anyone's fault, it was just unfortionate.

The Tea Party took Washington by storm in 2010, delivering the House to the GOP and ending the Democrat's Super-Majority in the Senate. Unfortunately, they did fail to oust the unpopular Harry Reid by selecting the goofball, and former Democrat, Sharon Angle, as their candidate. I will agree that she was a bad candidate and the establishment pick was plenty conservative.

Not so in Connecticut. I actually liked Christine O'Donnell. She was not a kook. She was a decent Conservative woman who happened to admit on Bill Maher's show (not friendly territory) that, in her teens, she had dabbled in witchcraft. We all do dumb things in high school; I joined a dance class hoping to meet chicks and then couldn't figure out why everyone thought I was gay.

Instead of attacking Maher for releasing the old tapes to demagogue her, the establishment poo-poohed *her* and forced her to respond on her own with her infamous career ending, "I'm not a witch," ad.

She could have won if Karl Rove had handled her the way he handled Bush when his past shenanigans came to surface. Instead, it was "oh what a terrible candidate! We're going to lose!" And so we did. Oops.

But still, the shellacking we gave the Democrats that year, with the party united, was amazing. However, all Obama did was double down on his policies. When we lose elections, we're expected to soul search then move left. When Democrats lose, they ignore it and move left.

And so the debt ceiling debate. In the two years Democrats had a super-majority, they kept kicking this issue down the road. The new Tea Party backed GOP felt that increasing the debt limit would only invite more spending, so they offered a simple compromise: spending cuts in exchange for agreeing to raise the debt ceiling. Obama wouldn't yield any cuts demanding massive tax increases or no deal.

Republicans started by asking for a nominal one hundred billion in cuts. In the end they got only marginal cuts to projected spending increases. Next, they accepted Obama's sequester proposal, which would be only further reductions in spending increases across the board, but to programs considered sacred cows by both parties. The deal did not see any real time cuts to spending at all and Obama got what he wanted in the end: an increase in spending coupled with a perfect chance to demonize Republicans over the issue, all the while advancing his class warfare narrative.

Let's put this in kitchen table terms. Imagine you are $16,000 in debt and you're trying to pay it off, and your spouse wants to add $10,000 dollars of new debt. You try and explain that you need to get out of debt and deal with what you've already spent. Your spouse responds by only spending $8,000 more instead of $10,000 more. Do you allow that to be called a spending cut? Why are we letting Obama get away with doing the same? Only in his case, the debt is sixteen-trillion and he wanted to spend some ten trillion more. The Tea Party only managed to shave off some two trillion from the increases in spending, yet we're supposed to believe that is a spending cut? No! It's taking a $16 Trillion debt and making it $24 Trillion over ten years. It is still a spending increase.

In response to our government's lack of seriousness about our debt problem, S&P downgraded our credit rating. Naturally, the press blamed the Tea Party, ignoring the reality that the downgrade occurred because the government authorized itself to spend $8 Trillion Dollars more over ten years, but dared call it a spending cut.

The very next day, my wife and I went to do a voter registration drive for the SLCOGOP. We got two registrations and hundreds of lectures. Everyone and their dog let us have it for what they saw as the "Tea Party Capitulation." Shortly thereafter, I saw fewer of the known Tea Partiers show up to County Committee Meetings and other local activities. I don't know how it was for other areas, but after the debt deal, the Tea Party seemed to just go away. The exception was Freedom Works, who greatly misjudged the public's appetite for deposing popular Senator Orrin Hatch and targeted him, while ignoring the opening they had in replacing Democrat, Jim Matheson in Congress.

To Hatch's defense, he's a very nice man. I actually really like him, even though I don't always agree with him. Most Utahns like him. He was never as unpopular as Bennett and with the anger over the failings of Bush further behind us, the anti-establishment mood fizzled out.

Hatch's opponents were decent men, but they failed to make the case to the public why he should be deposed. Then Hatch did something that was unbelievably stupid, and complained about Libertarians. He even went so far to allege that the party was being hijacked by the John Birch Society and that he was "dog gone offended" by their attempts to take *his* seat away-1. Does the John Birch Society (JBS) even exist anymore? The JBS was disavowed by William F Buckley, so I guess we were supposed to associate the Tea Party with them? Buckley also disavowed Bush though. I have only few beefs with Hatch, who has been usually solid in the past, but this divisive language was too much for me, so I offered Dan Liljenquist my support and begged him, "Unite us." He didn't. Instead, he ran one of the most infantile campaigns I've ever seen. Instead of using his time to articulate the reason he would be the best choice, he spent the primary season whining that Hatch would not debate him even though Hatch already had. Liljenquist spent almost no time with his boots to the ground. After reviewing his record, Hatch really was the better choice, even if he no longer thinks Libertarians should have a seat at the table.

Freedom Works, in the meantime, burned all of its political capital on trying to oust Hatch, even though he was the more conservative candidate. However, rather than going door to door to make the case, they sent out mailers with questionable claims about Hatch's record. The mailers were easily disputed by Freedom Path, an organization which appeared and disappeared with the Hatch re-election efforts, but had no problem causing suspicion of Freedom Work's claims.

Other Tea Party groups, such as Club for Growth, the 9-12 organizations, Tea Party Express, etc., seemed to stay far, far away from this race, while Freedom Works seems to have destroyed itself in Utah. It's sad, because we could have used them in the Matheson race which was just barely lost. Had they focused on helping Mia Love, it is not inconceivable we could have had the voter turnout necessary to finally win that seat.

I agree that Hatch has been there too long. Heck, he thinks the John Birch Society still exists! If it does, they are far from relevant to everyone except maybe Alex Jones, who is not relevant. But if conservatism is your cause, then Hatch was your man. It's hard to argue with an 87% conservative rating from the National Journal.-2. Last time I checked, that means he agrees with me 87% of the time. Therefore, I consider him my friend. It wasn't worth trying to chase out a good and experienced Senator who was doing his job! Unless you have a candidate like Mike Lee, who was an incredible candidate with a great campaign.

Meanwhile, the other Tea Party groups spent their capital trying to oust popular moderate, Governor Gary Herbert, due largely because of his acceptance of Obama's controversial Common Core. They failed to unite around a single candidate, and divided the vote against him in the process. There was one candidate who could have gotten into a primary with Herbert, Morgan Philpot. He was the challenger with the closest numbers, but he was beaten when another Tea Party backed candidate, David Kirkham, surprisingly backed Herbert after it was clear Kirkham would not win. In standing with the incumbent instead of the only viable challenger, Kirkham divided the opposition vote, thus nullifying it.

Although Herbert is a good governor, I happened to like Philpot's plan for eliminating the state's debt. Still, making the case we should oust an incumbent that is well liked is hard, and could only have been done with a united Tea Party. Instead, what capital they had fizzled out at convention. I have a few areas of disagreement with Herbert, but I do like him. He's a good guy and has done well managing the state, so I supported him for re-election after Convention, as I had in 2010. Although, I still believe it would be nice to have the state debt free. As good as Herbert is Philpot, I believe, would have been phenomenal. Unfortunately, the voters were too far divided amongst themselves to be anything more than a bothersome fly.

People told me at Convention that if Philpot had re-challenged Matheson they'd have backed him, but they felt that Herbert was doing fine and therefore didn't need to be replaced. Meanwhile David Kirkham's surprise backing of Herbert extinguished the anti-incumbent flame of the Tea Party, which subsequently has gone up in smoke. Well, at least in Utah its dead, so far as I can tell. I would love to be wrong on this, but see only a few small sparks of the Tea Party, where once there was a flame.

It's easy to attack a faceless phantom. Most of the Tea Party was wiped away in Utah in the 2012 caucuses and convention. Hatch did a great job organizing his supporters and getting them to turn out. The media had been attacking the Tea party as "extreme" for two years. The establishment joined in the attack and the Tea Party divided itself against itself. Now, the Tea Party is done and so too, is its agenda of fiscal responsibility and liberty. Since then, everything that the media dubs as "undesirable" has been described as "Tea Party." A recent Rasmussen poll showed only eight percent of the nation is willing to identify themselves as Tea Party, where once some forty percent had.

This had a wider cost to the GOP in Utah. With a Mormon at the top of the ballot, the liberal media was in a panic, proclaiming "demageddon" was going to happen and the last few Democrats in power here would be wiped out. However, as with the rest of the nation, the Tea Party and Libertarians stayed home. As a result, Jim Matheson was re-elected and Ben McAdams took the Salt Lake County Mayor seat. Nationally, Mitt Romney, who should have been a shoe in to defeat Obama, was defeated. Even wildly popular Mia Love went down in defeat, and literally, no one saw that coming.

Although, Salt Lake County had decent turnout, the rest of the state reported disappointing voter participation and the Salt Lake Tribune would, of course blame the Caucus and Convention system and closed primaries. In reality, that is elitist nonsense. The system is designed to engage ordinary citizens and give them real power in a way that a pure primary just can't. The real truth is that the party's infighting forced activists out, who then stayed home, which hurt voter turnout. There was such a scorched earth effort to eliminate the Tea Party that it will be surprising to me if any of them even attempt to come back. More and more these days, they are talking of forming a third party, but whether they stay involved with the GOP, or form a third party, as a faceless phantom they can never be given a fair shake by the press. Sadly, the establishment is clearly more interested in securing their incumbents than they are winning elections. The Tea Party, in contrast, is clearly reckless in their anti-incumbent efforts and have targeted perfectly good people which hasn't won them any favors.

Running around screaming, "rino, rino, rino," doesn't exactly promote the party unity we so desperately need. There were also a few of the Tea Party candidates were not that great, though the Tea Party's tendency to pick unelectable candidates has been grossly exaggerated. Still, I must agree with Karl Rove to the extent that we cannot have another Sharon Angle. However, I also agree with the Tea Party, in that we must not ever have another George W. Bush either.

The Tea Party's lack of central leadership was a fatal error in judgment. There was no unity behind a single candidate, there was a propensity to get distracted by social issues, it was chaos. Now, the term *Tea Party* is poison. The Tea Party must figure out what its central concerns are and focus on those issues alone. Fine tune the arguments you need to make. Calvin Coolidge said it perfectly, "I want the American People to work less for the government and more for themselves." This personalized the fiscal responsibility argument; similarly worded slogans would do the movement well.

Don't let the yellers and screamers become your candidates, and for the love of Pete, please make sure they have an IQ over 80. Sharon Angle must not *ever* happen again. I mean *ever!* Read Frank Luntz's book "Words that win." Install it in your brain, because overcoming the crass emotionalism of the left is no easy feat. Also, yelling at moderates only makes them angry with you, and like it or not we need them to win elections.

Remember, the ratio of Conservatives to Moderates is about 50/50 and Libertarians can make up another 5-10% if they are brought to the table, so let's stop terrorizing incumbents unless:

A) They are *really* _bad._

B) They are actually vulnerable and

C) You have a well-spoken and intelligent alternative (IE Mike Lee, Rand Paul, Ted Cruz, Marco Rubio, Allen West.)

The fact that the Tea Party rallied to people like Allen West and Herman Cain was lost on the media, who painted it as a racist movement based only on the fact that they dared to disagree with Obama. Meanwhile, to the media, opposition to Bush was heroic... whatever. The point is that the Tea Party must do all it can to attract female and minority leaders, which means competing with the GOP in outreach efforts. You have to have those numbers first, especially if you're going third party, which means boots to the ground, going door to door and meeting people.

Stay away from Donald Trump. I know he's not one of you but he is trying to engrain himself with you nonetheless. If you have any doubt that he is not your ally, then read his books, he's a progressive as well.

The central argument the Tea Party, and GOP for that matter, must cling to is a question; "Is a man entitled to the fruits of his labor?" If the answer is yes, then denying him any portion of the fruits of his labors through use of force is immoral.

Stay away from quirky and fringe issues. Utah's 2010 delegation got pulled into one man's personal beef with the party. He and his friends were suing the party, and through misdirection and demagoguery, convinced the delegates to elect his friends to the vice chair and secretary positions where they delivered non-stop embarrassment to the party in their pursuit of revenge for imagined slights against them. The incumbents in that race were great and I was sorry to see them lose. Most people I know, who are still involved with the Tea Party, regret voting for the buffoons in the vice chair and secretary in that cycle. Because of their buffoonery, the party tried taking the power to elect its leaders out of the hands of the delegates and leaving it to the State Central Committee, a measure I reject, but understand the motive behind it. Thankfully, this measure was defeated at the recent convention.

The biggest deathblow to the Tea Party, though, is really its failure to grow. Why are there no recruitment efforts? In business, they say if you're not growing, you're dying. I think the Tea Party makes that case. If the movement is to return to relevance, as I stated earlier, they must seek to expand. That means doing the hard work of getting out to neighborhoods and talking to people.

Now that I have thoroughly offended every faction of the Right, allow me to defend our media and entertainers, since no one else can be bothered to do that, ever...

References:

-1) Orrin Hatch 'doggone offended' by 'radical libertarians' trying to take away his Senate seat Read more: http://dailycaller.com/2012/04/13/orrin-hatch-doggone-offended-by-radical-libertarians-trying-to-take-away-his-senate-seat/#ixzz2M3np6iUW Accessed 2-26-13

-2) The 15 Most Conservative U.S. Senators — And You May Have Never Heard of No. 1, Jason Howerton http://www.theblaze.com/stories/2013/02/20/the-15-most-conservative-u-s-senators-and-you-may-have-never-heard-of-no-1/# Accessed 2-26-13

-3)   Voter   Turnout.   Salt   Lake   Tribune
http://www.sltrib.com/sltrib/opinion/55349346-82/election-turnout-voter-
utah.html.csp Accessed 2-26-13

Chapter 14: And When We Should Circle The Wagons, We Circle The Firing Squad...

I remember in the earlier part of the century, my friends on the left urged me to listen to Glenn Beck. If only more on the right were like him! He was willing to criticize Bush! My how times have changed! I finally broke when my grandmother recommended him. Now she's a survivor of the FDR years and a staunch Conservative. My far left friends and my grandmother agreeing on the same guy? Well he was going after Bush, as did William F Buckley.-1) Liberals loved that!

Buckley and Beck had a similar view of Bush. He wasn't a Conservative. Beck's "problem" (a good one to have) is that he approached Obama with consistency. Unlike the leftist Lame Stream Media, who suddenly became okay with everything Bush was doing when Obama was more of it, Beck's values didn't shift, so he became the enemy. Obama didn't change the direction of the country, as much as he forced the gas pedal to the floor and unbuckled all of our seat belts, as we began to zip toward the cliff. Beck became critical of Obama, so now conservatives loved him, while liberals hated him. Then, many on the GOP found that he wasn't a faithful Republican... worse, he's a moderate Libertarian. Shock! Horror! So now they hate him too.

Beck also began to notice some strange ideas and values being expressed by the President and those who surrounded him. Unlike Alex Jones, rather than employ a tin foil hat, Beck did something that journalists used to do: he investigated. He began to assemble damning footage of the Democrats saying and doing some pretty scary things and dared to air the footage in full context. The things we learned, not just about Obama but the Democrats, and some Republicans, were shocking, but Beck never aired anything he didn't have ample evidence to support. He even called out fellow conservatives when they got their stories wrong, such as the Shirley Sherrod case where everyone except Beck was claiming she had made racist statements to the NAACP. Beck found she was, in fact, telling a story about overcoming her own prejudices. So why is he so controversial?

Like Cleon Skousen before him, Beck has been the subject of a mass smear campaign that has impugned his character. Rather than going after the facts, his opponents just call him names, exactly what was done to Cleon Skousen. Far easier to call him a "whack job" than to counter the mountain of facts that Beck would provide his audience.

I do know the moderate establishment of the GOP doesn't like Beck or Skousen, but it's not just them. The establishment hates Rush, Hannity, Michelle Malkin, John Stossel, or anyone who represents the values consistent with the Conservative or Libertarian base of the party. The left leaning media blasts these standard bearers, the people who can actually articulate our message, and sell it and have made millions doing so. The Meghan McCains of the world join them in berating those who are the only people willing to explore the Republican's side of things. When people on our side go out and berate them, rather than defend them, it puts the credibility of the entire party at risk. After all, John Boehner hasn't exactly managed to sell our message, so why attack those who make a living doing just that? Who else is there who will defend our values, let alone promote them? Wolf Blitzer? Please...

You don't see Democrats lambasting Chris Matthews or Rachel Maddow, even though they belong in strait jackets. They won't distance themselves from that vile and disgusting Bill Maher who said far, far worse things about Sarah Palin than Rush ever said about Sandra Fluck. I'm sure there must be moderate Democrats who are embarrassed by CNN, MSNBC, or Current TV... Nope, no such thing as a moderate Democrat... You can always find Republicans willing to cap their own in the back of the head for ratings, but you never find Democrats willing to eat their own, and this is why they win elections and we don't.

I don't always agree with Beck, whose stance on video games saddens me as it belies his otherwise Libertarian values, but most of what he says is usually well researched and well backed. He is also refreshingly honest. When he does error, he leads with his corrections. I don't see that anywhere else. I disagree with other conservative media figures all the time, but on the whole they're good people and don't deserve the belittlement from their own that they often have to put up with.

Those of us on the Right have been bemoaning the liberal dominance and bias of the media for years. Yet, when we have a rising star on our side, we are sure quick to join the left wing media in smacking them down. How do we get our message out if those who would give it voice aren't defended and are instead made pariahs?

We've got to get better about standing by those brave enough to represent our side on the issues. So what if Democrats are offended by them? Democrats are offended by anybody who's not a registered Democrat, including people who are guilty of no other crime other than being a Christian, or a carnivore. They will always tell us who they're afraid of by attacking them mercilessly and trying to goad us into joining them in those attacks, an invitation we ought to decline. We cannot convince the masses of the righteousness of our cause by killing our own messengers. It sure as heck won't help us win elections.

Instead of picking up on the concerns being brought up by Rush, Hannity or Beck, we tried to run an election on the premise that "Obama's a nice guy, he's just in over his head." We also missed the memo that we weren't in power, except for Bush in the White House, when the economic collapse occurred and that Bush only vetoed three bills passed by the Democratic supermajority from 2007-2008, when the collapse occurred. I think that the public ought to know that little detail. Sadly, our party leaders never get out there to defend themselves, let alone our principals, so why berate those who do? How is this plan working out?

Moreover, the media is so in bed with the Democratic party that moderating all factions of the party will do no good, you will always be "too extreme" even if you fall in line with them one hundred percent of the time. They are fully committed to the end of our party. Maybe they want revenge because we kicked their butts in the Civil War. We should have learned that lesson in 2008. Remember, we nominated McCain because he was the token Republican that the media loved... until he was up against Barack Obama. Then all hell broke loose. Everything McCain said was deemed racist, no matter how innocuous, and every policy he proposed fascist and extreme.

The moderate establishment has got to recognize the media for what it is: the propaganda wing of the DNC. While we shouldn't engage in propagandizing the public in response, we should promote alternative media that will at least not treat us like the enemy.

-1) Buckley: "Bush not a true conservative." By Amy Clark, CBS News http://www.cbsnews.com/8301-18563_162-1826838.html accessed 2-19-13

Chapter 15: The Trouble On Immigration

We are a nation of immigrants, but let's be clear, the pilgrims were not illegal immigrants. There wasn't a country here and no immigration laws to violate. The pilgrims would lead to the conditions necessary for a country to be established. This red herring, that the pilgrims were, themselves, illegal immigrants, is a fallacy we're hearing now, used to justify treating illegal immigrants with a preferred status.

Other red herrings we hear are as follows:

-We need to be compassionate

-Our system is broken

-Opposition to amnesty is racist.

My response to this tripe is as follows.

1) Agreed, but no more than we would be with any other law breaker. We wouldn't grant a bank robber amnesty just because they tend to vote Democrat... wait, I better stop, I'll give the Dems ideas...

2) No it's not. We really just need to enforce existing laws uniformly for *all people of every country.*

3) Again, I believe in *uniformity of law*. No persons, groups, countries, creeds or political parties should get any special privileges at any time. Ever. Bringing race into this discussion is the ultimate red herring. It's

not a racial issue. It never was. It's about an immigration process that is equally fair to everyone regardless of national origin.

My mother is an immigrant, so her experience informs my opinions on this matter. It would surprise many that I am actually a proponent of a market based solution. Some opponents might call that an "open border," but I am of the opinion that everyone should be able to go where the jobs are. However, as a matter of practicality, this cannot work where the partnering countries are not open borders and free market based themselves. Mexico is neither and, in fact, has a very harsh border enforcement program compared to our own, "look the other way if they vote Democrat," policy. The mere suggestion that we ought to concern ourselves with the border is called racist.

Why is a one-sided open border impractical? Imagine you live on a farm. The horses decide to be nice and let the other animals into their pen, to share the food in their trough. The other animals come, but they leave their pens closed. So what happens when the horses' trough runs out of food? They can't go to the chicken coup because it's locked tight. If, however, all the animals on the farm opened up their pens to all the other animals, then all the animals would be free to go wherever there was opportunity and everyone would have equal access to all the resources.

Right now, Americans are hurting for lack of jobs. Meanwhile, Mexico and everyone else has their border locked up tight, so opportunities are scare. It is an unusual time to look the other way for people who are breaking the law, unfairly competing with legal immigrants and other legal residents for already scarce and vital resources. It is not, therefore, unreasonable to ask that immigrants come through the front door, rather than break the law and be "undocumented." That is *all* the right is asking them to do. By all means come here, just do so legally.

It is a massive straw man to call people on the right side of this issue "anti-immigrant." How else would my mother have gotten here? Or my Great Paternal Grandfather? Were it not for *legal* immigration, I could never have been born. That is true for most Americans. People calling folks like me, who are trying to take a practical approach to this, "anti-immigrant," are being misleading and distractionary. As I said in the last chapter, these days it's easier to just call people names, these days, than debate the merits of their argument. It is the same with the use of the term "undocumented." It is a diversion from the truism that immigration is a two pronged debate that diverges from a singular issue into two entirely separate issues: legal immigration and illegal immigration. I am ***very, very pro-legal immigration,*** but there are some eleven million people who broke the law to be here, who are creating an unfair source of competition for those who have followed our laws and done things the right way. Illegal immigrants hurt their legal counterparts, whether they mean to or not.

I am also confused as to how immigration has become centered on only Latinos. It's as if all the immigrants from Africa, Asia and Europe no longer matter. I mean, there are a lot of places people can migrate from, yet we only ever seem to discuss Latinos. I'm sure that is offensive to them, especially since more are here legally than illegally. We ought to be discussing illegal immigration much more uniformly than we do.

But here's my personal observation. Is it a coincidence that every single legal immigrant I know (including Latinos) are Republicans? If not, then we know why Democrats hate them and are looking to grant a special privilege to illegal immigrants. This while they are trying to scare legal immigrants by trying to debate the issue in broad strokes, rather than the nuance the issue needs because legal and illegal immigration are two separate matters.

Let me be clear, we want the best and brightest each country has to offer. There is a front door and I will meet you there with open arms and a voter registration form to sign you up as a Republican. Democrats meet you at the back door, tell ghost stories about "evil" Republicans and frighten you into registering as a Democrat, but let's cut past the nonsense. The arguments over immigration are entirely a battle for votes. Democrats don't care about anything else. It's all about dividing people into blocks that can be climbed up like Super Mario climbs the blocks to get to the flag. And like Super Mario, Democrats will have no problem breaking the bricks that get in the way...

Don't believe me? In the 1930s and 40s Progressives considered themselves a Christian movement, believe it or not. Today, they berate and belittle Christians as "anti-science." If you are going to let the Democrats make you a block, be aware that if at any point you cease to tow the line they will break you.

Examples: Christians

Legal Immigrants

White Southern Protestants

"Neo Cons," (Republicans who used to be Democrats)

Reagan (who was a Democrat before converting to Conservatism)

Anti-Communists

And more recently: Jews

All the aforementioned were, at one time, Democrats or Democratic constituencies. The latter still is, but is slowly trickling right as the Democrats become increasingly hostile toward Israel. In fact there was a ten point shift our way in the 2012 election cycle. I suspect that trickle will become a flow as the Democrats become more entrenched in the idea of Palestine, but that, I'm afraid, is a whole separate book.

Back to immigration, Republicans really dropped the ball allowing this issue to be demagogued, because as much as our constituents of legal immigrants and law abiding citizens will cringe hearing this: Amnesty, under the euphemism "pathway to citizenship," must be included as part of a compromise, in order to get this divisive issue off the table. While Democrats were changing the narrative and terms of the debate, we stood back and did nothing. As a result, we must deal with the consequences of letting the Democrats control the language.

Republican and Tea Party hero, Marco Rubio, was helming a plan which had a whole lot of compromise I think most of us could live with. Sadly, he allowed Chuck Schumer (D) to take those compromises and toss them out the window for a 1,000 page amnesty nightmare, which will not lead to the compromise Rubio promised us. At best, it is the 1980s amnesty fiasco all over again. Amnesty for Democrat leaning voters in exchange for the *promise* of secure borders later. We fell for it in the 80s, but we must not do so now. We must not allow the Democrats to continue to play this game. This must be the last time they are allowed a massive influx of Democratic voters. Period. The GOP controlled house must put forward a plan that will deal with the incentives to illegal immigration, not just pass the Senate Gang of 8 bill.

Furthermore, we ought to actually go out to Hispanic neighborhoods and actually talk to these folks. We must make sure they know we're talking about rule of law, an *orderly immigration process,* which will be fair to them and everyone universally, so that no one can be made to feel like we're picking on them and singling them out, just because El Presidente' says so. Getting to know our Latino neighbors might actually make them feel like a part of the community... and who knows, we might actually make some friends while we're at it. Assimilation is every bit as much our responsibility as it is theirs. As these immigrants, legal and otherwise, get to know us, they will discover we are not the monsters they've been told we are and we might be able to flip this on the Democrats. Then watch them build a fence so fast your head will spin, thus destroying their incentive to push for amnesty. We can't just capitulate on this issue and expect that Latinos will start voting Republican. We've never had a majority of the Latino vote and we never will if we don't actually work for it. Sorry, but again, that means boots on the ground, bringing cookies to new neighbors and inviting them to activities. Kind of like what church members do for new neighbors.

It needs be said, as we reach out to *all* minorities and youth, that recapturing the language is a must so that we don't find ourselves in this mess again in the future. Don't let the left get away with euphemisms anymore. Pointing out that someone broke the law to get here is no more dehumanizing than pointing out that someone ran a traffic light. The former is here illegally and the latter is speeding. Period.

What is dehumanizing, is looking to vulnerable illegal aliens as a source of cheap labor. Can't afford the insane price of minimum wage? (An issue I will explore in future books, I promise.) No problem! Hire an "undocumented worker," pay them a pittance and support illegal immigration, just as the Chamber of Commerce has, because they are cheaper than legal immigrants and citizen workers! If the left really cared about these people, they'd be writing all the time of the way they are treated, made to work in dirty, and unsanitary conditions and paid wages that no American would take. It's through illegal immigration that cheap industrialists get away with acting like it's still 1890, with no one willing to crack down because it's politically incorrect to do so. I wonder what would happen if the "undocumented" work force were to organize a strike? Would the Chamber of Commerce be so accommodating? Nope. Watch them build a fence so fast your head will spin, again defeating their incentives for amnesty.

What is dehumanizing, is the way the left uses Latino "undocumented workers" as political props. Tired of pandering to a center right nation? No problem! Wait at the back door and usher in a whole lot of new folks who have no idea what's going on and urge them to vote for your guy, on only the premise that the other guy is "racist!" An informed undocumented worker would vote Republican (I guarantee it) if they were told what the political battles in this country are really about and what's at stake. Then again, that is true for every voter.

The debate needs to center on rule of law, not crass emotionalism, demagoguery and name calling. Right now, we need to assemble a plan which won't let the Democrats have a field full of uninformed new voters. So we should follow the following principals.

1) Verifiable increased border security. I mean if the Chinese can build a wall, why can't we?

2) Deportation of all criminal illegal aliens, including and especially identity thieves.

3) No welfare, or other social benefits until fully nationalized.

4) No voting until fully nationalized.

5) Must take classes on American Civics, not taught by the Department of Agriculture, but by people who actually like the

country, such as the Thomas Jefferson Center for Constitutional Restoration or Hillsdale College.

6) A guest worker program, including reasonable (as in low and affordable) fees to enter the program. $5,000, like in Utah's HB116, is too much and undocumented workers cannot afford it.

7) Guest workers cannot be paid less than market value for that job. No more using them as cheap labor.

8) Green Card after five years on this plan, or two if they serve in the military.

9) May apply for nationalization after ten years on this plan, or five years in the military.

10) Deport Sean Penn and Barbara Streisand.

I've tried very hard to find a balanced approach here. Our government is insisting on amnesty in some form or another, and our refusal to defend our position, *as order on the border,* has led to the necessity of compromising, even though I keep hearing that immigration is actually pretty low on Latino's radar. Like everyone else, the economy, education and kitchen table issues are much more important-1). It is here where the conservative message should be able to win over votes. After Five years of Obama, shouldn't it be clear that liberalism isn't working? It would be quite clear, if we were to let people know an alternative exists.

I am willing to compromise on this issue, but there is one more thing I want. As I have said, I am an advocate of uniformity of law. I do not agree with laws which favor one group over another, the way Jim Crow laws did, because no laws should exist which grant preferential treatment to *any* groups, no matter how you justify it. Therefore, Ted Kennedy's immigration act must be repealed. This bill granted preferential treatment to unskilled, poorly educated laborers from third world countries, in the name of helping the under privileged. But we know that this was really about getting cheap labor, you know, to help those poor billionaire Democrat donors get around the ever increasing minimum wage... Imposed by Democrats. At the same time, Democrats get to build a collection of uninformed voters that can be easily frightened into voting Democrat. It's time for a uniform policy which grants preferential treatment to *no one.*

So fine, pathway to citizenship one last time, but, dog gone it, secure the border first and quit using immigration to acquire poorly paid slaves and easily frightened, uninformed votes. Fair? Well, not to legal immigrants like my mom, but I think it's the best we can do with the way things are in Washington. However, if you really want to turn this issue on the Democrats, it's time to go meet with immigrants and minorities and include them in your community. No other outreach program will be as effective, of that I am sure. Then, once they are voting with us, watch the mask come off the Democrats as they reveal themselves as the racist dictators their history clearly shows they are.

-1) Immigration Is Not The Most Important Issue For Hispanic Voters; Chiqui Cartagena And Leading Marketers Debate The Issues Which Will Drive Hispanic Voters http://www.huffingtonpost.com/2011/10/04/immigration-not-the-most-important-issue_n_993918.html accessed 3-1-13

Chapter 16: Revisiting Video Games: A Gamer's Response to Beck's Stimulus/Reward Theory

A lot of chapters in this book are either expanded blogs, or thoughts too long for blogs. Blogs are often a reaction to the news. I have always been very frustrated with certain pundits, on the right, who have responded to recent news by locking onto video games as the source of all of society's woes, despite any evidence to the contrary (which is always ignored.) They continue to press this issue, as the left presses the guns as the problem, when neither are. I cannot stress enough that *things* are not the problem; individuals making evil choices are the only cause and should be the only recipient of blame. Sandy Hook was Adam Lanza's fault, not the Bushmaster fire arm, not Call of Duty. Focusing on guns and games distracts from the discussion we need to be having, which is mental health and bullying. Nearly all of the recent mass shootings have been perpetrated by people who turned out to be mentally ill, and many past shootings were triggered by the bullying the shooter was suffering from.

There is a book called *Control,* and much of it is about firearms. I happen to agree with most of it, but there is still a rather sizable section dedicated to video games. The author, again, is a man who I normally agree with, but not on this one issue. I am disappointed by Glenn Beck's spending a massive section of the book going after video games. Most folks my age play games. Most of us grew up playing games. It is this behavior we see, on the right, that pushes my age group away from Conservatism because it sends the message that the right wants to take our stuff away. Never mind that the left actually does promote censorship, it is only helping put further distance between the 35 and under crowd and the Republican/Libertarian/Constitution coalitions. Not a good thing.

Video games are so common in today's world that it should be as expected in the American household as say bread or mayonnaise... except I hate mayonnaise so that may not be the best comparison, unless we can compare mayo to all those Guitar Hero games. There's always too many of them and they ruin an otherwise good idea... or sandwich... Still, video games turning up in the home of a criminal should not be a surprise to anyone any more than a roll of toilet paper being present. In the case of Call of Duty, at present, there are fifteen million people playing some form of that game or another. It was bound to turn up at a criminal's house at some point, so too would pants and a pair of glasses, so common are games.

For a while, it was getting harder to listen to Beck, because data contracting his thesis is widely available and easily found in a simple Google search if anyone is willing to look. There is no link between video games and real life violence. -1) Yet, Beck is completely unwilling to hear counter arguments. On his 2-22-13 show, he claimed that his daughter has found all kinds of horrors that, allegedly, no one knows about in video games that his book will "expose." Well, unfortunately, his book falls for many of the same tactics anti gamers have used for years to attack my favorite past time, including tactics he attacks the Obama administration for using against guns (IE using limited outdated and bias studies done during the nineties) to make his point.

I've been involved with defending video games for a very long time. I want to talk about these exposés, because this discussion has actually already been proven a waste of time by newer, more thorough studies, including the fact that millions of gamers play games and only a select few have gone on to commit mass murder. Actually, nothing in Beck's latest book is new or shocking. Predictably, he goes after specific games, which are market failures, or outdated games that no one plays anymore, that will have no one come to their defense because they either bombed, or are so old that no one cares. What Beck details, and what he withholds concerning these lucky few outdated, irrelevant titles are designed to draw your attention away from guns and place the blame on video games. This isn't a great way to reach out to young Libertarians and young adults, by the way. Again, it is a perfectly legitimate argument to say "I grew up playing games, and my criminal record is squeaky clean!" That is 99.999% of us! It is the ultimate scientific test of a product's safety, and when the vast majority of gamers can accurately make this claim, it renders all arguments to the contrary moot no matter how many "scientific studies" you dig up from 1990 BCE.

One of the reasons I do admire Beck is because he encourages you to do your own homework. I will echo that, but add that you will find a study to counter every study done on this subject. Real life experience ought to be the telltale indicator. Since the United Stated Department of Justice reports a decline in violent crime in the last twenty years, then one ought to conclude that if video games have anything to do with violence at all, they are suppressing it. Granted, this is conjecture, just as the book *Freakanomics* attributes this decline to abortion and *Roe v Wade* using exactly the same conjecture I'm about to.

It seems like what children are playing encourages lethargy, and I cannot deny that there have been plenty of days I have spent playing video games, rather than exercising. Ergo, people are sitting on the butts getting fat, but they are also staying off the streets and out of trouble. At best, the latest and newest actual scientific studies behind links to video games and real life violence are rife with contradiction and are, therefore, inconclusive. -2) Remember what Ayn Rand said, it is very important to making a logical argument: "Contradictions do not exist. Whenever you think you are facing a contradiction, check your premises. You will find that one of them is wrong." There are millions of gamers, and only a few seem to go crazy. The fact that the vast majority of gamers are well rounded, decent individuals, contradicts the premise that games cause violence. Therefore, I propose the premise that video games cause real life violence is a fallacy.

The tactics of the anti-gaming crowd have been the same since I was a kid and Mario dared smacked Yoshi to make him eat a turtle. Time for another list!

1) Bias Sample Fallacy: Allege scientific links between games and real life violence using often incomplete, easily manipulated controls and biases to get the result desired. Or site studies done

twenty some odd years ago that have since been undone by newer studies. Again, this is exactly the same tactic Beck attacked President Obama for: the use of the discredited 1990's survey alleging "40% of guns sold without a background check." I must stress again, however, for every study establishing a link, there is one which establishing that no such link exists. This which establishes contradiction and invalidates the premise. Most of the newer studies I have seen indicate no link, but with so much contrary data out there, one must look to real life, rather than labs for answers. When we look to real life, we can see that there are 15 million people playing Call of Duty, and *only* Adam Lanza went on a rampage. This suggests other factors should be looked at for Sandy Hook, such as the fact that he was a known mental case.

2) Appeal to Authority Fallacy: When you can't find a scientist to agree with you, find an authority figure (often just some nut who claims to be an expert) to make your case. For *this* topic, this is usually Florida attorney Jack Thompson, or more recently Lt. Colonel Dave Grossman, who claimed that the military uses video game simulators. True, but they're not playing Call of Duty all day. Our military is pretty trim, most gamers are… well… not. Sadly, there is some truth to how gamers are portrayed in South Park's *World of Warcraft* episode. The use of simulators in military training is neither new nor the primary nor only method of

training. They have customized situation simulators, some for as mundane a situation as driving or flying an air craft, but the anti-gamers will claim that the games we play for fun and the situation simulators used by the military are the same. Based on that fallacy, many conclude that since the military uses games for conditioning people to kill, all video games make all people killers... Well, I suppose if you're using video games or simulators, as would be the case for Colonel Grossman, whose job it is to train military people to kill, it is natural that this would be the prism you look through. I use video games to experience the Hero's Journey, as 99% of us who play games for recreation do, but in the purview of anti-gamers the 1% of gamers who are mentally ill (Adam Lanza) represent the majority. That math seems backward to me. The only thing gamers are trying to kill is *time*. Note: the term nut is a cut at Jack Thompson, not Colonel Grossman. I respect Colonel Grossman, but believe has a skewed view of the matter considering his profession. Also, I am a fan of Beck, but I believe has a skewed view as he is a father gazing through the prism of a father concerned that his son may not be making the best use of his time.

3) Appeal to Fear Fallacy: Find specific games as "shocking examples," that are ancient and no longer relevant to gamers that no one will defend, such as Doom, Wolfenstein or Manhunt. They may also target games that were market failures like Manhunt 2,

Postal 2, the latest Duke Nukem, or games that are best sellers, and are current but the content is often greatly misrepresented to make them seem worse than they are.

4) Burden of Proof Fallacy: Ignore all data to the contrary.

5) Questionable Cause Fallacy: Assert that because games can be found among a criminal's possession, games must be causing the crime.

All of these tactics drove me nuts as I read this in Beck's book. I had to add this chapter just days before this book went to press, but since I pretty much know these tactics by heart, I want to take a moment to dispel some of the nonsense that I fear will inevitably end up in every book like "Control." I don't know why people on the Right feel compelled to use the political tactic of deflection whenever something they like is attacked. It seems to me that Beck rushed his book to publication. While the first half of it is great, the second half is sloppy and easily picked apart. It is more like a pamphlet put together by the NRA's Wayne LaPiere than something I'd expect from Beck. Although I am a member, the NRA is on my naughty list because, although I appreciate that they should not be vilified for a crime they had nothing to do with, just because you don't want to be the villain, doesn't mean *somebody* has to be labeled as a villain. These tragedies are the result only of individuals who choose to do evil. There is nothing else to blame, but I digress.

I'd also like to assure the anti-gamers reading this that there are conditions in the market which suggest that video games are not a healthy market, and so again, this argument is moot but thanks to the second half of Control, I think I need to reiterate it... Again... I agree that some of the following games I am about to write about *are* inappropriate for children, but the free market ought to decide the fate of the video game industry. There is also a rating system in place to help parents make informed choices when selecting titles for their children. You can read more about the rating system at www.esrb.org. There is no further action needed from government or activists.

Call of Duty: (Current title, best seller, content highly exaggerated. Played by over 15 million people worldwide, only one mass murderer known to have played it, that being Adam Lanza.)

Allegations: Extremely violent, gives points for massacring people, used to train military to kill.

Extremely violent: Only about as much as any war movie.

Give points for massacring people: Not true, however there is one entry in the series where you are an undercover spy that has infiltrated a terror cell in Russia which strikes an airport. The sequence is integral to the game's story, but does not encourage, or force, or reward your participation. In fact, you later play as a survivor of the massacre out for revenge. Games tell very involved stories today, arguments exist as to whether it is better to use movie sequences (or cut scenes) to drive the narrative, or real time participation. Call of Duty uses the latter, but there are no shades of gray in this game. You are America, or Britain against the Nazis, Axis Powers, or Russian, or Islamic terrorists. It's the sort of game that the Right would love, but for the alleged link between the game and Adam Lanza. Of course, the only source citing a link between Lanza and Call of Duty was an obscure article posted by CBS, which was retracted due to the fact that much of it was conjecture without any source citation. I read it, but the article has since been scrubbed from the Internet. To date no solid evidence exists that Lanza did what he did because of Call of Duty, only that he played it.

Used to train military to kill: Patently false, the simulators used to train police and military are not the same as consumer video games. This is a bold faced lie. Some may have video games in the rec-room, but playing on a dual analogue controller is not mechanically comparable to holding, aiming and firing a rifle. Aiming and firing a rifle is actually easier than using dual analogue sticks in video games. I still suck at Call of Duty *and* target shooting, but I've done enough of both to say that they are just not mechanically comparable.

Doom: (Past best seller, no longer relevant, the latest entry in the series was released in 2004, almost ten years ago. Doom was popular in 1993 but has since been overshadowed by games like Halo.)

Allegations: Horrifically violent, inspired Columbine.

Horrifically violent: For its time perhaps, but you're fighting demons not people, so who cares?

Inspired Columbine: While the shooters, Eric Harris and Dylan Kleybold, were known to have been fans of the game, there are some facts oft forgotten. This horrific school shooting happened at the height of the assault weapons ban, so the ban did not do any good, and Doom was already an outdated game at the time of Columbine. Like Call of Duty now, these were just two kids out of millions who were playing Doom during its heyday. Only two went on a shooting spree, the rest went on to live normal happy healthy lives. Moreover, most experts agree that the events at Columbine happened because the two were shunned outcasts who were frequently bullied. Interesting that Beck completely ignored the study by the Secret Service a year after the massacre, which showed a stunningly high number of these types of attacks happened in response to bullying -9. Allegedly, the two boys were often tormented due to their assumed homosexuality -10. I don't know if they were gay, I don't think anyone does, but I do remember I had a really nice business coat and people used to give me hell for wearing after Columbine, for allegedly being involved with Harris' and Kleybold's "trench coat mafia." No such group existed, that I am aware of, and it wasn't a trench coat... Oh look at that... facts do matter... So much for Doom being the problem. When you look into it, bullying was the problem. Much like how the problem with Adam Lanza turning out to be poor mental health. Anyway, Doom is irrelevant today, no one is playing it now and so it is an easy target, because like a dead man can't defend himself, dead games can't either.

Duke Nukem: (Former hit of yester-year, current bomb.)

Allegations: Excessively violent, gratuitous sexual content

Duke Nukem, as a franchise, may have been an issue. However, the excessive violence is against mutant space pigs not people, as I recall, though I have not played these games in ages. While there is certainly inappropriate for children adult content in the older titles, one must remember that the last successful entry in this series was released in 1996. You read it right, 1996. The latest entry in the series, *Duke Nukem Forever,* was a commercial and critical failure, selling only about half the numbers that 2K Games had hoped to sell, -15) meaning it's not baby-sitting your kids, though this game was expected to be a massive mega hit, it just wasn't.

Manhunt/Manhunt 2/Grand Theft Auto: (Market failures, current title best seller respectively)

Allegations: Excessively violent, teaches kids to become serial killers by awarding points for killing people. The latter is lambasted for teaching violence in general but especially toward cops.

All are true for these disgusting and pathetic games, however, no one played Manhunt or its sequel. Neither were commercial successes, and both are obscure, irrelevant, and not symbolic of what the industry is like. Again, this is making it an easy target because no one plays them, so no one cares to defend them. I won't defend this game or Grand Theft Auto, as both franchises are excessively violent. However, to date, no evidence exists positively linking either game series to real life violence. Manhunt, as a series, died an early death because it sucked. More recent GTA games have already significantly scaled back their violence, so GTA's developer, Rock Star, is already responding to market pull rather than government pull. Both games carry an M rating, meaning for adults 18+. An AO rating is therefore not necessary, as neither series is meant for kids, nor marketed toward them, and as I recall, 18 years old is an adult.

Mortal Kombat: (Current title, but interest is waning. Respectable sales but not the kind of numbers we see with Call of Duty anymore. This series will probably be forgotten in a few years.)

Allegations: Horrifically violent and sexist.

Well actually I am tossing the sexist argument on the table on this one. No one else but me is talking about this, but I must because, as a martial artist, I study with a good number of female fighters who can whoop me in real life. I have developed the opinion, from my real life experience, that martial arts inspired video games are often disrespectful to those powerful women who deserve to be portrayed in video games; not as the glorified, almost nude sex goddesses, as they are portrayed in Mortal Kombat, but as the amazing and powerful artists they are. This aspect of the game has come to really bother me especially in more recent years.

The violence of the game is so ridiculously over the top, however, that it becomes comical. While I wish that some aspects of this series would grow up, past the fifteen-year-old boy mentality, I don't see any evidence that this game is causing kids to kill each other in real life. Show me the kid who killed his friend by ripping his head off with his spinal column intact, then maybe I'll consider joining protests against this series. However, kids don't play this game, this series is only bought for nostalgia for the 90s anymore. It's gameplay is dated, it still sells reasonably well but not enough to have franchise owner WB (as in Warner Brothers) kicking out a new entry to the series every year the way we get a new Assassin's Creed like clockwork. It's hardly the cultural icon it used to be and probably isn't worth fretting about, unless you're willing to demand a more respectful approach be taken to its female fighters. Similar complaints about Tomb Raider have caused Laura Croft to be re-designed to where she is much more realistic and much more respectful of women. Instead of being reduced to a sex object, Laura now can be a symbol of female empowerment, as opposed to fifteen-year-old boy excitement. Mortal Kombat needs to have that evolution now too. It's way past time, but in the meantime, no one could possibly confuse Mortal Kombat for reality.

Oblivion (Elder Scrolls IV): (Current title, top seller)

Allegations: Excessively violent, contains full frontal nudity.

Both patently false. When this game launched ten years ago, the game received a T rating. It was only as violent as Lord of the Rings, no more. However the PC version of the game was modified by a hacker, creating an unauthorized code which removed women's clothing. This was never approved or created by the developer Bethesda, ever, and could not be done on the Xbox or PS3 versions of the game. It could not be done on the PC without the user developed hack. Regardless, the ESRB re-rated the game from T to M for mature as a precaution, causing the controversy that anti-gamers cite to attack this brilliant game.

Skyrim (Elder Scrolls V): (Current title, best seller)

Allegations: Excessively violent, encourages homosexuality

This game has a great free market economy and can be used to teach capitalism, if you really wanted to. The game contains multiple means of making money and exploring the work-profit relationship. The government is very limited. The game's content can get a bit violent, but there are not gallons of blood spraying everywhere, though the game does contain occasional animations of decapitations and the like, which are just too much for kids. However, kids aren't playing this game. It is an extraordinarily complex game, and those who are growing up playing Angry Birds aren't going to have the attention span necessary to learn to play it. This game's level of violence was likely inspired by the ESRB's re-rating of Oblivion from T for Teen to M for Mature because of the aforementioned user hack. I'm sure Bethesda decided to just go for the M for Mature rating, rather than risk having to spend all that money recalling, re-labeling and re-shipping the game again, like they had to do with Oblivion. Likely, they put in just enough violence in there to push the game over the T for Teen line into M for Mature territory, but no more. This game is no more violent than the latest Hobbit movie, in reality. There is no nudity or sex, though user hacks exist for the PC version on the *Nexus* Mod site. There is a limited number of eligible NPCs available for said marriages, but once you put on a specific medallion, the player is allowed to choose one of a select number of NPCs as a life mate. The game does not define marriage the way we do though. It's an alien world (Nirn) with alien customs. Still, there's nothing promotional about the games' marriage content. In other words, you don't have to marry at all. However, if you happen to be a gamer who is gay, that option is there for you. Frankly, I'd like to see the family life aspect of this game expanded. It's actually a nice step forward, but it's not as varied as it should be. It's also disappointing that the game makes you adopt children, rather than allow you and your wife to have children on your own. It's also sad that those children stay kids indefinitely. I am glad that this option was included in the game, but it's hardly worth writing home about.

Thrill Kill: (Never released.)

Allegations: Most disturbing and graphic violence ever depicted, teaches kids to kill people

Umm... that might be a great argument... *if the game ever actually came out.* The game was scrapped eons ago, it never saw the light of day, but its preview keeps getting dug up by anti-gaming activists as a means to "expose" just how "horrible" and "shocking" video games are.

And now I want to address another title specifically brought up by Beck. Postal 2.

Postal 2 was another game which is old (2004) and was lambasted by critics. I am unaware of a console version of this title and *Computer Gaming World* gave the game a score of zero. -11. This games metacritic score (a scoreboard by a user community rather than professional critics) gave it 50% out of 100%. What can we conclude about this title based on this data? Simple, the game is not and never was popular, largely because the content was racist, homophobic, bigoted and too violent even for gamers. Critics and players alike hated this game and it bombed. It is hardly your child's baby sitter as Beck alleges.

There is also one game Beck mentions, *Soldier of Fortune*, which I do not feel qualified to comment on because I actually, believe it or not, have never heard of it. It may be a big hit with excessive violence, for all I know, but I can only comment on games I have either played, or researched. Right now all the First Person Shooting gamers are playing *Call of Duty, Battlefield, or Halo*. No one is talking about this game. Perhaps it's excessive gore was an attempt to get attention, but considering that no one I know is talking about it, it must have not worked. In trying to look it up, I found there's a lot of media called *Soldier of Fortune,* but there hasn't been a game by that title since 2007. Gamespot gave the game a lukewarm 7.5/10 -12, while 1up.com gave it 5.5/10 -13... doesn't seem like a mega hit to me, though I couldn't find sales data. Still, this game does not appear to be being played now, so I reiterate, it's hardly you're kid's baby sitter. If there is a newer title he is referring to I would like to know.

I want to stress, I usually agree with Beck, but believe him to be wrong on this issue, painfully. Even his co-host Stu, and his colleague on the Blaze Andrew Wilkow, have both pointed out areas of disagreement on this topic. I feel their points, valid as they are, were ignored in this otherwise excellent book, *Control.*

I recommend read the first half but don't bother with the second. It is nowhere near as well researched and, as I keep pointing out, often uses the same tactics he criticized Obama for to make their point.

I worry that Beck may have fallen in with Jack Thompson, a left leaning Republican attorney who thinks he's a conservative but isn't. Thompson is just another commie nut case who thinks the answer to all life's problems is government regulation of your entertainment. If there is one valid point they have, however, is that studies do show that we are exposed to a lot of violence while growing up. What those studies don't talk about, however, is that this is nothing new. Before there were games and movies, there were revolutions. Heck, the left has a nasty habit of dragging the Rich and Royalty out into the public square and very violently executing them in public. There are well documented wars and rumors of wars, and before all that we used to feed Christians to the lions and watch gladiators battle each other to the death, hacking limbs and heads off for entertainment. Our entertainment is only a reflection of the violence we see in real life and throughout history. No video games inspired Nero to burn down Rome, nor Lenin to have the Czar killed, nor Hitler to kill six million Jews, or Mao to starve some seventy million of his own people. Violence is a human problem, one that comes from the very darkest corners of our own nature. Art imitates life, not vice versa and I do believe that games are a modern art.

In the end, there is a rating system for a reason. Many games are not meant for kids and are not marketed toward them. Parents need to be involved in what their kids are playing and watching to be sure, and none of the aforementioned games are for kids. They shouldn't be playing these games, but to the defense of the Gaming industry, they are marketing their products toward people my age, who make up the bulk of gamers today. We, the gamers of the world, are over 30 and aging fast. Which brings me to another reason this debate is not worth your time. The age of the gamer has created an economic shift in the industry that is likely to spell doom for the electronic hobby in the next 3-5 years. I will explain.

I remember back in 2011 when relatively debt free Nintendo, who historically had always managed to profit (even when lagging behind the competition in sales), lowered its income forecast by 300 million dollars.-3 Clearly, it was a rough year, despite selling 80 million Wiis globally and some 5 million Nintendo 3DS'. Since their respective launches, the software sales has been mediocre at best. The launch of the 3DS was a disappointment as well, though the subsequent price slash helped the 3DS's prospects stabilize. The recently released Wii-U, however, is being met with an unusual amount of skepticism for a Nintendo product, even by hardcore fans. All told, Nintendo's sales have plummeted some 40%-50% in the last couple years, a disastrous number. They have only recently begun to recover, but if sales do not pick up for the Wii-U, that marginal recovery will be short lived.

The prognosis for the Big N is not good. Games are being delayed or cancelled left and right and many industry analysts are focusing on Nintendo's many recent "mistakes." The thing is, Nintendo hasn't done anything unusual for their business model. The Wii is about seven years old now, five years into the N64 and GameCube software sales dropped dramatically and interest declined as Nintendo prepared the next system. What is unusual though is that the Wii-U's sales have not been good, nowhere near what the expected sales were forcing Nintendo to cut sales projections.-4)

Many have said that Nintendo's fortunes are the result of overpriced and underpowered machines, with lackluster launch line ups. However, the 3DS' sales model followed in the footsteps of its predecessor, launching at a larger price than the DS, which launched at a larger price than the GBA. Both the GBA and the DS had lackluster launch lineups as well. The DS also faced a monumental challenge, as a more powerful competitor (PSP) was hitting the market shortly after its launch, the 3DS' direct competition (PS Vita) didn't launch until much later, leaving the 3DS a large amount of time alone on the market. However, with the GBA and DS Nintendo Crushed Sony's efforts, despite being a weaker platform, with a weaker launch line up.

Some have said that the rapid price drop of the 3DS spells doom for the system. It is true that rapid price cuts, not just for Nintendo, but everyone, is usually a sign that they won't dominate this generation, but there are other factors at play and the focus on Nintendo belays the deeper problem... It's not just Nintendo in a state of deep hurting. What may be a surprise is to learn that

Sony's sales have recently tanked as well. Now. the PS3's price tag was very hard to overcome until recently. The PS3's sales have not been anywhere near as strong as the PS2 was, yet despite this and the recent 12% dip in their sales -5), no one is declaring doom and gloom for Sony. Though, to be fair it's software sales have been stronger than Nintendo's, but the company's sales are still in decline.

Microsoft has also had reduced sales, as have Konami, EA and Capcom's, whose sales are down an alarming 37%-6). Worse yet, Square-Enix is on its deathbed and countless experts have proclaimed the death of the western localization of JRPGS (Japanese Role Playing Games, my favorite genre.) These days it seems like if your game isn't Call of Duty or Assassin's Creed, you're sunk.

There are a lot of factors contributing to this problem: the advancement of the smart phone as a gaming platform, the novelty of motion gaming all but worn off (The PlayStation Move is all but dead), lack of compelling software... the list goes on and on... But the real problem that no one wants to talk about, is that people aren't buying games. All but the absolute must haves are collecting dust on store shelves. Why aren't people buying games? Well, many of us hardcore gamers are now in our thirties and forties, we have families to feed and it's hard to do that in an environment of perpetual 7-9% unemployment and a real inflation rate estimated to be about 10% -7). These problems are not going away and are not likely going away anytime soon.

For those of us nerdy enough to follow economics, like myself, we know the real reason this is happening. Government is borrowing and printing money in numbers we have not seen since the Weimar Republic. Obama's exacerbation of Bush economic policies have taken the bad situation Bush left us in and made things far, far worse. The more money in the system, the less value it has. The less value the dollar has, the less gas, food, utilities and other basic necessities we can afford. The more we have to spend on the basic, the less superfluous money we have to blow on games, DVDs, Blu Rays, music and comics, all areas of industry in a state of decline. It is not helping that what job growth exists almost always comes with a deep cut in what people are making now, as opposed to what they used to make prior to being laid off.

And get this, if Obama gets his way and gets a "balanced" approach to economics (which amounts to increasing the nation's credit card without paying any of it off) and taxes get raised even more, then there will be even less money to blow on extras. For those who believe he'll only go after the rich, let me remind you his hero, (the notorious racist) Woodrow Wilson, promised that only the top income earners would ever have to pay income taxes, and then only 1%. Within a few short years, everyone was paying income taxes and the top earners had to pay over 70%. Look at your paycheck, is the government taking money out of it? Now imagine a scenario where they take even more in the name of "balance."

Smart Phones have a lot of what we gamers call shovelware. Junk games in other words. There are a couple of fun, little, addictive titles like Fruit Ninja and Angry Birds, all of which are great when you're trying to kill five minutes. None of these games come even close to being as good as a full handheld experience. So why are Smart Phones outpacing the handhelds? Well, in today's market Smart Phones are a necessity, while dedicated handheld gaming units are a luxury. When money is tight, the luxury items fall to the waste side.

Look, no one I know doesn't want a 3DS or the Playstation Vita, a Wii U or the upcoming Playstation 4. My friends who have played my 3DS have all found reports of it being "underpowered" to be a gross exaggeration. Since launch, I have gotten some twenty different games, and with the exception of Zelda, all have given me a near-X-Box like experience for almost half the software cost. Why pay $60 for Dead or Alive, when the 3DS version looks and plays almost as good for $40 and has the bonus of being 3D without glasses? I think the 3DS has a great line up.

The Playstation Vita failed to even register on the market, and IGN even recently featured an article suggesting trading it for a Kindle Fire-8) Most people I know wanted one, but couldn't afford it. Technically neither could I, but I am just that hardcore of a gamer. Also, my wife and I have been unable to have children, so we don't have the responsibilities that most people our age do. But this phenomena has caused the video game industry to start circling the drain.

Since most folks who would play games can no longer afford them, games aren't selling, causing losses to the developers, development teams getting laid off and studios closing their doors. After that, there are no games to attract players to the new systems, so those new systems don't sell. Even the gaming press has begun to notice, as IGN writer Jared-IGN put it recently, "Money is hard to come by these days for many people. I often wait for Xbox Live Arcade games to drop to 400 Microsoft points before I make a purchase. You can call me a cheap bastard, but as a grown man with bills to pay, games often have to sit on the sidelines so I can keep a roof over my head."-14

People can't buy new machines or software, so the drain circling continues. Once in a while a game comes out that sells by the truck load, but those hot sellers are getting fewer and further between as the cost of living goes up, while people's disposable income continues to shrink. If people didn't have to worry about how they going to pay for their next tank of gas, than the Vita and Wii-U would have been a smashing success. I predicted the PS Vita being doomed to the this fate a couple years ago in a blog I wrote. It's the reason why I feel the hardware manufacturers should have delayed new hardware as long as they possibly could, while focusing on cheaper and better games instead. The less expensive the entertainment, the better it will sell. There is a reason why, in spite of Netflix, there is always a crowd around the $7.00 Blu ray bin at Wall Mart.

I predict the PS4 will have similar problems to the Wii-U and the Vita if the economy has not improved significantly by the time it launches. It will have a strong initial showing, but I'd bet heavily sales will quickly taper off. With Obama digging in his heels and doing nothing that doesn't take more money out of private hands, it is unlikely that the PS4 is going to fare much better than the Wii-U in the long haul. "How can you say that?" You ask, "The PS4 pre-orders have already sold out! So have the Xbox One!" So did the Wii-U, I know, I tried to Pre-order one. I had an easier time snagging a PS4 pre-order! It was only because Walmart ordered a number of extra units, in addition to their pre-orders, that enabled me to buy one. Given the state of the economy, I anticipate a similar fate for the upcoming PS4 and Xbox One.

My guess is that saving the gaming industry will require a new president, one who will back away from this tax and spend insanity and reinstate a laissez faire economy. Historically, laissez faire *has* worked. Calvin Coolidge did it, Reagan did most of it and in both cases, after two years of cleaning up the mess of the Progressives before them, the economy rebounded and people started buying stuff they wanted, but didn't need, again. The policy of laissez faire lead to the boom of the 20s, the prosperity of the 1980, 90s and most of the early 21st century. I promise you if we hold the line on spending now, with a free market oriented president, we will prosper again... after 2 years of cleaning up the mess...

In total, we're looking at the potential for as much as six or seven more years more of this since Obama was re-elected. It will go even longer if the Democrats maintain power in 2016. It will get worse if the Democrats are not defeated even sooner than that in the 2014 mid-term elections. Economic polices matter. Government spending matters. Tax policies matter. The great tragedy is that by the time we can get around to fixing the economy, it may be too late for the video game industry, rendering arguments about whether or not video games make people violent a complete waste of time.

Maybe you're glad of the bad news I delivered, but as a gamer, as someone who grew up playing these games and turned out just fine, who loves to play games on the rare occasion my wife lets me... and as someone who went to the Art Institute with the intent on using that to get into video game development, I am looking at this situation all aghast.

Of course, after playing Bioshock Infinite, I saw it made clear that many in the gaming industry think that Obama's policies are good. They also seem to think that people like me who revere the founders, love God and find virtue in faith are the problem. I cannot help but think that, in many ways, the folks running the game industry are like the folks who were on the ill-fated train ride in Atlas Shrugged. It is their support of these bad policies that are leading to their own demise. I expect Hollywood, too, will follow in short order as disposable income becomes a thing of the past. It's hard to feel any pity for them at all, as the train of progressive thought crashes head on into the train of economic reality. It's just more proof that altruism, not guns or video games, kills.

References:

-1) Ronald Bailey, Reason Magazine 2-13-13 Killing Pixels Is No More a Cause of Crime Than Reading Comics Turned Out to Be http://reason.com/blog/2013/02/12/killing-pixels-is-no-more-a-cause-of-cri Accessed 3-2-13

-2) Links Between Video Games and Violence 'Inconclusive' spong.com,
http://spong.com/article/23206/Links-Between-Video-Games-and-Violence-Inconclusive Accessed 3-2-13

-3: Nintendo Loses 25.5 Billion Yen by Richard George www.ign.com
http://ds.ign.com/articles/118/1184697p1.html accessed 7-29-11

-4) New Wii is no fun for Nintendo, Wall Street Journal.
http://online.wsj.com/article/SB10001424127887323701904578273120108154866.html Accessed 3-3-13

-5) PS3 Sales Dip by Colin Campbell www.ign.com
http://ps3.ign.com/articles/118/1184708p1.html accessed 7-29-11

-6) Capcom Sales Fall 37 Percent
Jim Reily www.ign.com http://games.ign.com/articles/118/1184739p1.html accessed 7-29-11

-7) Inflation Actually Near 10% Using Older Measure, CNBC
http://finance.yahoo.com/news/Inflation-Actually-Near-10-cnbc-357695506.html?x=0 accessed 7-29-11

-8) My Break up with Vita, Bill Roberts, www.ign.com 1-28-13
http://www.ign.com/blogs/smoothzilla/2013/01/28/my-breakup-with-vita accessed 3-3-13

9) Out of order due to data added later. Boodman, Sandra G. (May 16, 2006). "Gifted and Tormented". *The Washington Post*. Accessed 5-5-13

10) Out of order due to data added later "The Community: Columbine Students Talk of Disaster and Life", *The New York Times*. April 30, 1999. Accessed 5-5-13

11) "Postal 2 PC Review". Computer Gaming World. Accessed 5-5-13

12) Gamespot.com accessed via search 5-5-13

13) 1up.com accessed via search 5-5-13

14) Jared-IGN, **Could a Virtual Console Subscription Service or Better Pricing Help Nintendo?** April 30th 2013, http://www.ign.com/blogs/jared-ign/2013/04/30/could-a-virtual-console-subscription-service-or-better-pricing-help-nintendo/ **accessed 5-5-13.**

15) "Take Two Estimates Lowered After Disappointing Duke Sales". Gamasutra. 2011-07-05. Accessed 5-5-13.

Some citations are out of chronological order as they were added later.

Chapter 17: Common Sense Education

I'm lucky in that as a child, growing up in Utah, I had several great teachers who at least respected the vision of the Founding Fathers. In the 90's, the collapse of communism was still fresh on everyone's mind. I don't recall Jefferson or Franklin taught as philanderers as they are now, but as high minded philanthropists whose idealism would lead to the Constitution, the eventual abolition of slavery, and the foundation of a nation where people of various different backgrounds would come together and prosper in freedom. In a nutshell, that is the Jeffersonian view, but today the only thing school cares to tell you is that he had slaves, therefore he was worthless as a human being and so his ideals and values are not worth considering. Only Karl Marx and Martin Luther King were ever virtuous. Well, that's my takeaway from college anyway.

Much of what I saw in college was more subtle, I didn't have the in-your-face communist propaganda we sometimes hear rumblings about. Most of my teachers at my college were fairly balanced, but some would shut down my projects as "too controversial" if they were politically themed. Meranwhile, students who did projects centered around global warming, or global do-goodery, or bashing Fox News were encouraged and allowed to proceed. Do a project celebrating the Tea Party and explaining why the phenomenon was a good thing? Nope, had to scrap it and start over.

There were only two major issues I had with college, first is that English classes devolved from being about sentence structure, to writing essays about other people's (usually anti-western) essay. If my grammar is bad, at least you now know why. Some of those essays we had to write about were blatantly anti-white, rife with a racism all their own. I have to applaud my teacher though, because when I would use my essay to deliver a scathing response calling out the author for their blatant racism, my teacher did not complain, and did not defend the original essay... but was surprised that anybody could see the essays the way I did. Still, I got my grades.

The other was in my art history classes, where we were expected to believe that because early Christian artists used the solar disc used by ancient Egyptian artists to identify their sun deities, that Jesus is just another Pagan Sun God. This art class tried awfully hard to push the discredited theory that the story of Jesus is the same as Horus, or Buddha. Anyone with even a mild familiarity with ancient mythology knows that to link Jesus with other mythological pagan gods is more than a little bit of a stretch. Those selling this theory go out of their way to re-image the ancient myths to more closely match the story of Jesus. In example, they claim Horus had twelve disciples and a virgin birth, neither claim is true.

Horus was the son of Isis and Osiris. When Osiris was killed, Isis copulated with his corpse and conceived Horus. Horus also had an incestuous relationship with his uncle as well, which doesn't sound very Christ like... I could go off on these various so called "links" for eons, pointing out how radically different the stories are from each other and how, in reality, the story of Christ is distinct and unique in the ancient world. But that is an entire book, which I will write someday, if colleges continue to pretend that their students are incapable or reading an encyclopedia. Also, I don't remember Jesus mediating under a tree, like Siddhartha Buddha, for twenty five years but I digress.

Today, we are definitely seeing some bizarre trends in education; from trying to dispel Christ by linking him to pagan gods, to whom he bears little to no resemblance whatsoever, to videos of school children singing praises to Barack Hussein Obama "mmmm, mmmm, mmmm," to kids being dragged out of a class room to protest Scott Walker, without their parents being consulted first, to college professors offering students free credits for their class if they participated in the(bogus and violent) Occupy Wall Street movement. Something is very, very wrong in education today. Let's not pretend that the institutions of higher learning are not hostile toward religion and western values, and especially Republicans.

The proof of our dire need for reform is in the pudding, when you factor in the fact that our test scores are in serious decline. Now you have the President talking about building government run work training facilities. That, right there, illustrates the prime differences in the view of education between the left and the right. You see, on the right, we believe Education *is* a facility meant to teach kids basic survival skills, as well as work skills. College is about teaching them the skills specific to the trade, or industry the child wants to work in.

I'm not a leftist, so I won't try to pretend that I understand what they think the purpose of education is. There's plenty of chatter out there on what the left's beliefs concerning the purpose of education are. To date, no one can explain them to me clearly, in a way that doesn't make education sound like a propaganda instrument of the DNC. I don't want to accuse, but I do find it curious that so much time is wasted on social studies that haven't helped me out any. Studying the problems of society is usually a wasteful subject, especially since so many of society's problems are really only divisive political wedge and bludgeons, most of which the ordinary person is powerless to do anything about. I know, because I am one of those ordinary people, and when I tried to do something Democrats and Establishment Republicans called me names, hoping I'd sit down and shut up. Instead, I wrote this book.

With so much focus on frivolous problems that society has, it seems to me that it has been lost on educators that we're not living in the 60s. Still, leftists continue to behave, and teach, as if we are. Society is ready to move past the 60s, yet people like Nancy Pelosi, Harry Reid and Barack Obama cling to those days, as do a lot of educators, *exacerbating* whatever social problems do still exist in the process.

I came out of school clueless on how the economy works, without any sense of direction, or discipline. I had to learn how to manage money the hard way. I am still am finding it hard to break some of the habits from my college years. I thank God every day that I had such amazingly patient parents, that I met such amazing people like Dan Thatcher, Sifu Steve Thatcher, and Dr Glenn Kimber, who each contributed greatly to straightening me out. Otherwise, I would have probably ended up occupying Wall Street too, because that is what school and the news were telling me to do. Thanks to them, I learned critical thinking skills, history and economics, all kinds of things that are not taught in school but should be, especially Kung Fu, but we will get to that later. I cannot thank the Lord enough for the influence of these amazing mentors. They don't always agree with me, but they are the ones who got me thinking and more importantly, questioning.

It saddens me to watch as my nieces come home with their heads full of nonsense about how racist and awful America is instead of knowing how to balance a checkbook, or to avoid credit cards, or anything else that's useful. Even sadder is the fact that they never question any of it in class. My niece, Jaq, can go on for hours about Martain Luther King, but has no clue who George Washington is. Jaq does asks her family a lot of questions though, so it's not hopeless. I don't know why there is so much Anti-Americanism in the schools these days. It seems to me like we are committing national suicide by encouraging students to hate and despise their own country. When kids are coming out of college with no clue how to work, but plenty of skill in protesting issues they do not understand, we can only reasonably conclude that education, as an institution, is failing.

Commonsense reforms must take place in order for us to raise the standard and raise a generation capable of functioning in society. Here are the reforms I believe we must push for.

1) Deemphasize social justice and social studies at large. Society's problems are a political prop to keep us divided and have little to do with the individual's day to day life.

2) Re-implement history in its place with equal parts the good America has done, and the bad and what we have learned from our mistakes.

3) Allow for Martial Arts Studies as a physical education option. They do this in China, their kids are a lot more fit than ours and it has helped reduce bullying.

4) Allow teachers to custom tailor their lessons to the needs of the individual student, rather than expect the student to conform to a standardized curriculum; flexibility is needed, since no two people are exactly alike.

5) De-emphasize "new" math, except in cases where students express interest in a field where it will actually be needed. All through High School and college I would ask my math teachers "when will I need this in real life?" They would always assure me it was needed, yet advanced mathematics never clicked with me because I never had a real life need for it. Emphasis should be placed on the "old math" because that I do use, daily, diligently and at length as I follow the economy.

6) Teach science in a manner not hostile toward religion. Schools need to let parents and children decide for themselves whether or

not to believe in God. Teachers and professors have no place belittling people's deeply held personal beliefs or promoting atheism.

7) Require that if a subject is going to be taught from a political prism, that both the left and right wing view be presented fully and fairly, so that students may decide for themselves what to believe.

8) Teachers and Professors must be disallowed from involving students in protests, marches or causes that the teacher and professor believe in but students might not. Education should not be about promoting political ideology. Students can organize for themselves if they want to, but in my experience don't, unless "nudged" by the teachers. Teachers should not be allowed to deliver that nudge at all.

9) Less federal involvement. Like I said earlier, teachers must be able to be free to custom tailor the lesson to the needs of the individual student. This is best handled on a local level.

10) Less homework. Kids need to have time for their family.

11) Teach both Keynesian and Classic economics, as well as Austrian Economics, and make sure students have a clear understanding of how the economy works... especially the negative consequences of Keynesianism.

12) Make sure they understand the consequences of debt and how to balance a check book.

This chapter isn't so much a compromise we could offer. The fact is that the Democrats have ruled over education with an iron fist for eons, and the reality is that something isn't right when we spend billions on K-12, then even more years of our lives in college, only to end up now needing job training facilities. I want the Democrats to explain their vision for education, because mine is that we use education k-12 to give students the basic skills they need to survive the adult working world and then college should be about giving them the specific skills they need for their ideal career.

We're already hearing rumblings of doctor shortages. Any idea why? Eight years of a very expensive schooling, when one lawyer can muck it up for life? Seriously, one malpractice suit, and the poor Doctor is done. What's the incentive to put so much work in to something so easily lost? How much of that eight years is wasted on social studies that don't have anything to do with helping a surgeon understand how to remove an appendix?

How about engineers? I hear we're shy a few of those as well.

The things I am about to say will be controversial to both sides of the isle, but I beg you to hear me out. I had a rough time in K-12. I was frequently bullied and really hated having to be there. That's not to say I wasn't interested in learning. I've been reading non-fiction books for years, studying whatever science interested me (space in particular), looking for deeper answers than what Sunday school could provide, but I cannot say I got much from high school itself. I was (am) socially awkward and never really fit in. While most guys were into sports, I was into art and I can't say that absolutely every class I took ended up benefiting me in the adult world.

All my life, I wanted to write, to draw and tell stories in video, especially in movies. As of now, creating videos is a part time hobby for me, but I wanted it to be my career. It would have been beneficial if, when people asked me what I wanted to be when I grew up, they didn't laugh me off when I said I want to make movies. Instead someone should have said, "okay then we need to get you into the following classes." Unfortunately, when I was in high school, video productions was brought in as a pilot program, and attracted mostly people who were looking for easy credits and spent the class time mocking me, rather than doing anything constructive. Different circumstances could have better prepared me for college.

College was a also a disappointment. I could only afford to go part time, so it took five years to get an associate's degree that is going to cost me some $70,000 to pay back. Dealing with that bill, in specific, is the reason I am publishing this book and why I need it to sell. In the real world, the Associates Degree is worthless... but it didn't used to be. I now know the ins and outs of many Adobe software products, but it is still not enough to land a job with the film industry, who won't hire anyone who doesn't have a BA, let alone a Right-winger without one. Heck, go online and you will find that you need a BA to flip burgers at McDonalds these days.

There's two points I am getting to, the first is that it shouldn't have taken so long, or cost me so much to get an Associates. I can think of more than a handful of classes that I had to take that I don't feel were necessary for helping me to understand the industry, or how to operate within it. At least 25% of my classes were more ideological dribble than anything to do with art. I hear it's worse in other colleges. By eliminating the mandatory nature of the social and ideologically driven courses, we can reduce the amount of mandatory credits needed for a degree, thus shortening the length of college and reduce the cost of it at the same time. I worry Democrats would not support such a move because it would mean most people would not opt into the ideologically driven courses, thus causing the funding for such courses to dry up. I argue that if they are not useful to the career path I am interested in, than I should not have to fund it, unless I want to and as you can probably guess by now, I don't.

The second point is that education has gone up in cost as an investment, but down in real world return value. The BA is the new High School Diploma. It was a big deal when my dad got his ASC. It opened up opportunities for him that would eventually lead to him making a decent living wage, though the sour economy would lead to his recent lay off as well. Today, you say "I have an Associate's Degree," you get, "we really need someone with a BA." This is a serious problem which makes it so that many students are unable to get a return on their investment. I need to go back to school, to be sure. I want to course correct my life, get into tax law so that I can defend Conservatives being persecuted by the IRS, a Constitutional lawyer, and later a judge. This is a much more realistic life goal. It took me until my 30s to realize I had a better chance of following that path and succeeding, than trying to make movies with a $70,000 Asc. But how do I justify going back to school when it cost me $70,000 to get the Associates? Will I make enough money to offset the cost of the bill after getting a BA in law? Can I even get the student loans to do it, when I haven't been able to pay much on my existing loans?

If you listened to Occupy Wall Street, many of them expressed their outrage over exactly this, though their anger was misplaced. They were mad at the banks who had funded their education, rather than the colleges who charged them the arm and the leg in the first place. I am mad at the college. They absolutely failed to deliver on the promises of a lucrative career in the arts. Besides my loans were taken over by the government anyway, so there you go.

This point, I believe, the left and the right should agree on is this: The cost of education is exploding and college savings accounts do nothing to offset it, due to inflation. When you graduate college, you will have a mountain of unmanageable debt, with a degree with far less value today than it did even just a few years ago. If you do not have at least a BA, you may as well drop out of college, or even high school. Your value in the work force is that diminished.

We need to examine the causes. I believe it's greed at the Universities, personally. Many of the Ivy League schools have billions in their bank accounts, and collect fiendish tuition fees at the same time they collect grants, and subsidies from the Federal and State Governments. Yet, to date, no one on the left or the right have questioned the massive wealth the Universities have. While

I am a capitalist, I do think there is enough competition in the market that prices should be falling. I don't understand why school is just getting more and more expensive, but for the fact that, thanks to subsidies, they don't compete.

The growing cost of education needs to be addressed. Democrats always just want to throw more money at the problem. Obama's recent education reform proposals illustrate that. The plan basically calls for granting larger loans to students going to colleges that have a higher score with the government. I strongly suspect that score will be biased in favor of the Ivy league schools who have more resources than poorer schools. This will only exacerbate the cost of education, piling more money in the hands of a few Ivy League schools, so that they can continue to ignore competition from less wealthy schools.

In contrast, I want to understand the problem, then once we know what the cause of the dramatic increases are, do something about it. For instance, if the schools are going to charge their students an arm and a leg for tuition, fine... but then maybe they don't need government subsidies. Maybe, without the subsidies, they will have to compete in the market. Suddenly students will start weighing costs and choose their schools based on affordability, not some federally mandated score board (which is more likely to reward schools for producing Democratic voters, than people who can operate a calculator.) My plan would cause the colleges to have to adjust their prices based on supply and demand, rather than ignore the market because of subsidies.

Lowering the cost of education will only increase accessibility, especially to poor and minorities who cannot even think about college. The increased affordability and accessibility will go miles to lead women and minorities out of poverty, unlike Obama's proposals which will only reduce access for the poor and minorities. Trust me, Obama's plan means granting decent student loans only to those going to the more expensive Ivy League Schools, who will inevitably be at the top of his proposed charts.

On the K-12 front though, I have not even a clue as to what the driver of increased costs are, but I do see some ways we can save money on the long term. One would be replacing the text book with a tablet PC. The first one the student gets, the state would pay for, but the parents would have to sign a form accepting responsibility if it gets lost, stolen, or broken.

The cost of printing the full color text books is enormous. Deploying those books as an ebook instead would dramatically cut the costs for the schools, so while there would be an upfront cost to upgrading our education system, we can reduce costs quite a bit in the long term. This will also make it easier to keep current with the latest and greatest text books, and we wouldn't have to spend money trying to get these books back from the students at the end of the year, or replacing damaged books.

I believe we have excellent teachers; I am tired of hearing people on the right saying "we need to do something about our teachers!" It is No Child Left Behind and Common Core that are binding their hands. To try to blame the teachers for a situation created by an out of control "standardization" is ruthlessly unfair. We need to untie their hands and allow them to unleash their creativity on the class room. You can't exactly standardize education without ignoring the needs of individual students. Teachers must be free to customize and adapt to whatever challenges they are presented with. As of now, they are not.

I have a lot of friends and family involved with education. What is their number one complaint? The lack of interest that parents have in their own children's education. This has got to change. Recently, Utah's Legislature tried to reduce the need for sex ed in public schools and the public pitched a fit. Why? What parent wants to have to teach their kids about sex? It's embarrassing. But did any of those parents stop to ask how the teachers feel, having to teach this uncomfortable topic to the kids, on behalf of the parents who ought to be more responsible for their kids? Did any of them consider that sex ed does nothing to prepare them for a job and costs an arm and a leg? Or the fact that it seems to do more to encourage teenage promiscuity, than curb it? Is Education for preparing your child for the adult work force, or is it a babysitting service?

To many parents education has become a free babysitter. That attitude is negatively impacting their children's future. Parents who are disinterested in their children's education will have children who are disinterested in their education, and in the end we will have more kids susceptible to a life of crime, misery and poverty. There is nothing a teacher can do to prevent that. It's your job as a parent. Parenting requires an active role in your child's life.

These musings are just a place to start when asking the question of what can be done to improve education. This area is one that is in deep trouble, when it is producing Occupy Wall Street Protesters, instead of an eager and ready workforce, the industry is in deep trouble and needs some pretty serious scrutiny for us to even begin to understand what the core problem is and how to fix it. Where the compromise has to occur is that everyone needs to be at the table, this is an all hands on deck matter that needs immediate attention. Education must get cheaper and produce better results. It need not produce more Democrats.

Chapter 18: Hands Off My Medicine!

Obamacare has got to go. Already, the cost of insurance is increasing, not decreasing, and given that I went from a good paying job to a situation where I will be likely to make just slightly more than what is about to be minimum wage (thanks to the reckless Obama administration), I will likely drop from taking in about $1,000 per check, after insurance, to $600-$700 before insurance. Thus, when insurance costs are taken out, my checks may as well be coming from McDonalds. The devastation caused to my family and I, both in the reduction in income, plus the further reductions caused by the Obamacare mandate, is going to seriously reduce the quality of life for my wife and I.

It took me years of hard work to get to where I was, when I could afford to finally have health insurance. Unfortunately, the Obama economy forced our client to demand a significant cost reduction in order to renew the contract. That price reduction meant that reorganizing the company was unavoidable. I loved that job. That company was absolutely wonderful to me, and while I am enjoying my new job, the work that I do generally starts at about $10.00 an hour. This was a good wage in the year 2000, but thanks to the inflation we have experienced in the Bush and Obama years, it is now table scraps. With the cost of insurance exploding to almost $300 per check from my last plan, when $10 an hour equates to about $600 per check after taxes, what will a $300 per check plan do to my quality of living?

Sure, it's nice to have insurance when it's needed, but believe it or not, I only recently signed on to an insurance plan. I usually just paid out of pocket and avoided the hospital as much as possible. I don't know why so many uninsured individuals are drawn to hospitals. Perhaps it's lack of education. Hospitals are the worst place to go when you have the sniffles. The cost of a hospital visit can easily exceed a thousand dollars for the sniffles, whereas the local insta-care, or even your Dr's office, wouldn't exceed $150 for an uninsured visit.

Moreover, there are rumblings of free market based solutions that I really like. A few years ago, Walgreens was talking about opening up a small Dr's office in their store. For a nominal fee, say $25-$30, they would treat the sniffles. I don't know what happened to the plan, but I liked the idea. If Walgreens, Wal-Mart, Target, etc., all jumped on board with this, imagine how much cheaper doctors's offices would necessarily get, since they would be forced to compete with the cheaper options.

And why not? They all jumped on board with $4.00 prescriptions. The idea may have been abandoned, since it was several years ago that I heard these rumblings. It's possible that current economic conditions couldn't allow for such innovation today, due to shortage of Doctors willing to work for what would inevitably be a smaller pay check. We are experiencing a shortage of Doctors, we glanced over that in the previous chapter.

Another innovation that seems to be gaining traction is the health savings plans. But the rapid rate of health care cost increases are likely to make the health savings plans something that must be done in addition to, rather than instead of insurance plans.

There are many contributors to high healthcare costs. The problem with the government involvement in this issue is that everything they do is making things worse. Doctors get bogged down by more and more paper work, which takes time away from their patients and costs them time (which is money) to process. The ease of getting insane judgments against doctors, which can be life destroying, and the government's insistence on only paying doctors a fraction of what they are worth through the government programs, thus deferring the remaining cost to the rest of us. Then there are those who simply do not pay their bills. The losses that the medical industry experiences with those folks are deferred to the rest of us.

Obamacare does nothing to solve any of these problems. The reality is that it's going to make things even more expensive, if only for increasing the government bureaucracy that doctors have to deal with. The program will likely lead to a single payer plan, which will be even more expensive and deny services to those who they don't feel are a good investment, as similar programs do overseas. Harry Reid has already suggested a Single Payer plan to solve the problems caused by Obamacare. Single payer plans are always justified by the increasing costs of healthcare reducing accessibility, yet no one ever asks the question of "why don't we implement a plan that will decrease costs?"

First of all, make it so that it doesn't take eight years and $100,000 to get a doctorate. Don't let Medicare and Medicaid short them on the bill. Implement tort reform and watch the number of doctors in the market explode. That increased competition in the market will help create an environment where the doctors will have to lower prices to compete. Then implement the plans Walgreens had discussed a few years ago, the healthcare savings plans, and remove the barriers in the way of drugs falling into the $4.00 fill category. Next, allow for cross-state competition among insurances and you will introduce competition in to the market like never before, thus lower prices.

There is no need to force the cost of insurance up by requiring them to supply $10.00 a month contraception that most people can afford on their own, and those who can't can always go to their local Planned Parenthood. Though $10 a month for anything from condoms, to the pill, doesn't seem like an extreme cost to me... just lump it in with your grocery budget and maybe not buy as much soda... But such mandates force companies to either take that money away from cancer patients, or increase their premiums.

Insurances should not be required to cover every little detail of your medical life. A lot of health is just maintenance. I agree with the left that we need to do better about teaching nutrition. Where we may disagree is that I think China is remarkable for its full embrace of martial arts, we should as well. It seems like we're the only country in the world that doesn't take martial arts seriously.

Perhaps I am overstating the case, but it seems like England has fencing, Japan has Karate, Korea has Tae Kwon Do, China has Kung Fu, Israel has Krav Maga and France has calling foreigners rude names. What do we have? I don't think Ipad counts as a martial art, besides it's made in China... with Kung Fu. The point is that all of the aforementioned countries have something that, at least in the eyes of a foreign outsider, has universal appeal in their country and something that keeps people rooted in their traditions, lore, history and physical activity. America needs a martial art, or several.

Having a national love for something like, say Hung Gar Kung Fu, the style I study, would keep even the fatties healthy. My doctor is always shocked when my blood work comes in, "how are you not diabetic?" He will ask, and I will enthusiastically reply, "Kung Fu!"

I'm not saying that the government should nationalize a martial art and provide free lessons. Rather, I lament that we, as Americans, seem to think of Kung Fu as something cheesy to be mocked. The powers that be should work to promote this as a physical activity to help encourage a healthy lifestyle, communal unity and as a solution to bullying. After all, how likely is the school jock bully to try to beat up the school nerd if the nerd can drop him in just a few short moves? It is working in China, and while I abhor communism, this is one aspect of the country I greatly admire. Perhaps if we could see more Kung Fu in the Olympics? Perhaps if we would create a sort of national sport, or past time around martial arts... However it is accomplished, if you want to decrease obesity and encourage healthy living, this is the awesome way to do it and it doesn't require government investment per se', just promotion.

If ever I were to run for office, as dorky as I would appear, I would be advocating for a martial arts program in our schools as an alternative to PE. Watch all the school nerds sign up while being laughed at by the school jocks, until that first fight where the jock gets walloped while trying to stuff the nerd into the locker. Suddenly, a new respect for martial arts, the nerds and people at large will be found as the jocks sign up, and are taught the moral discipline they lack in football. Bullying will fall sharply, people will be healthier and that too will drive down healthcare costs.

These alternatives will be much cheaper than the prescription written by Obamacare. If Democrats actually care about the people they represent, then these are the compromises which should be readily acceptable to both sides. Teach people correct healthy principals and remove the barriers to cheaper healthcare and demand will go down, lowering prices. Meanwhile, supplies will increase, lowering prices. Healthcare problem solved.

Chapter 19: The Apologetic Unapologetic Apologist In Conclusion

I have tried hard to be approachable and to be the guy who is always cordial, regardless of the faction that the person I am speaking to belongs to. I have spent the better part of the last couple years calling for party unity before finally giving up on everyone. Post-election, there have been a few who have been at the wrong end of my wrath and I do feel I owe these people an apology. It is not for my lack of awareness that we all need each other to win, but my frustration that factional loyalties are such that no one is able to look beyond blaming the other faction. As someone who has ridden the fence between the factions most of the way, I have had an outsider's view of things that I think has caused me to become hostile to the very people who I am trying to help.

I must say that while I firmly reject collectivism and Progressivism, it avails us no good to run around calling Obama a communist, which I have done; though I have only meant it as an observation of his personal beliefs and not intended to be a belittling of the man. The time I have spent as a grass roots activist has taught me that people don't respond well to such, even though all reasonable evidence points to it being true. Thus, I must apologize to anyone I offended in making comments like that, though I still suggest studying history and you will start to understand the links between Communist ideals and Progressive ideals. It is an historically accurate observation to make, just be aware that people on the other side of the isle respond to that the way that we react when they call us Nazis.

Along those lines, while the Nazi platform does have more in common with the Democratic platform than the Republican platform, and while the Nazis, like the Democrats, believed in a massive nanny-state government (for Germans). And while it is historically accurate to remind people, when necessary, that Nazi meant National *Socialist* German Worker's Party, that they were not free market folks. And while it started as a largely Catholic movement, it later abandoned its Christianity in pursuit of a bizarre neo-pagan style belief system... calling Democrats Nazis is also not helpful.

Although Republicans are far friendlier to Jews lately, that the Democrats leading the fight against the Nazis is a point of history that should not be lost on us. They keep forgetting that we freed the slaves, let's not do to them what they do to us by forgetting what good contributions to history they have made, even though we may feel they are precious few in number. Ideally, neither side of the isle should use the "other N word" on each other. I have been guilty of calling Democrats Nazis. I apologize and promise I won't do it again except to point out National Socialism *is Socialism* and eschews the Free Market principals which guide the Republican Party.

I have been especially angry with the Moderate wing of the GOP. While I stand by my arguments I made in this book, and I do believe it is time for the GOP to part ways with Moderate stalwarts like John McCain, Lindsay Graham and a number of others, who have been licking the boots of Obama for far too long. The media likes McCain because he is willing to stick his thumb in the eye of the Conservatives, but when he was running against Obama he, too, was deemed "Bush/McCain," "extreme" and a "racist." Yet he, like Romney after him, actually ran very respectful campaigns until Sarah Palin went rogue and actually started taking Obama to task. Siding with the Democrats all the time does not a Moderate make. Rather, it makes it more difficult for Republicans to win elections when their own party is rife with "mavericks" willing to throw the entire party under the bus. Notice, as I restate my complaint, a word I have avoided? RINO. I have not used it, but have the word Ann Coulter used to describe Libertarians. Unlike Ann, I do apologize for it here.

While I am angry about the election results, (this should have been a cake-walk) I am more upset with the fact that the reality of the election results is lost on some factions of the GOP, who are only focusing on changing demographics. In truth, when you look at the actual birthrates, we're all in decline, and nothing is going to change unless we open the floodgates and deliberately choose to alter the demographics of our country with open borders or amnesty. Otherwise, if nothing changes now, in time nothing will change based on current birth rates, an issue the media is avoiding. As tragic as it is, *no one* is having children. The replacement rate is so low that it ought to be a crisis, as there will not be enough new workers to pay for the social security of the Baby Boomers. Generation X, my generation, is likely at even more risk, as we have even fewer kids than the boomers did having us.

This issue isn't s racial one. It's a simple truth that all races across the board, tragically, have very low birth rates. These startlingly low birthrates are not high enough to maintain the stability of our current welfare state. It is on this fact that we need to be working together to ask the big questions that need to be asked.

1) Is it morally right to take money from a younger generation to float an older one?

2) If so how do we make the welfare state sustainable?

This book is not out to answer those questions, rather, to establish the need for us to get past our emotional and reactionary ways, so that we can come together and look at answering those questions. As the welfare state expands, the security and the stability of the private sector is beginning to retract. Now, there are fewer workers to tax. It is so bad now that even local governments are beginning to retract. My home town of Tooele recently had to lay off 29 workers and shut down the Deseret Peak Complex (basically the local rodeo.) While people on the left immediately began to blame Republican budget cuts, the reality is that there are fewer working citizens here now than there was a few years ago, therefore, you cannot collect as much in taxes. Energy Solutions had been the major employer out this way, yet they suffered massive layoffs (in the interest of full disclosure, my father included). The company I had been working for was a company I adore. I greatly miss my team, my boss, my customers. Yet, the sour economy created a bad environment for our client who desperately needed a cheaper rate. The only way we could afford the cuts the client demanded was massive restructuring and I was swept up in that, getting laid off.

Nothing would make me happier than getting a phone call right now from my boss saying "guess what? Our client wants everything back the way it was! Come back to work for us!" But even though the news focuses almost exclusively on the occasional good economic news, our growth rate is less than 2%, our unemployment is close to 8%, 15% if you look at total unemployment (U6) at the Department of Labor. Our Labor Force Participation rate is at an all-time low at 63%, and go figure I couldn't find a job that paid anywhere near as much as the job I lost. I am grateful to be employed at all though. Many have no job at all or have been relegated to part –time.

This isn't about the debate between the good life and the good enough life, this is about a very real state of decline. The reality that we, as Americans, do not have the sort of quality of life we had grown accustomed to. In our comfort, we began to feel entitled, and in that entitlement, we elected leaders who promised us all a free lunch. But there is no free lunch, and the drying up of both the private and public sectors that we are experiencing are indicative of a very real need to solve the problem caused by our debt, much of which is caused by our welfare statism.

It is imperative that a unified right rise up to meet the challenges of our economic and political environment, rather than seeking a fundamental change to America. We need to stand together to arrest to political pendulum and calm the storm. We will never have the media on our side; it does us no good to suck up to them, we should ignore them and those who sponsor them. We have lost on key social issues, but can still work out something so that the consequences of that failure will be less painful. We need plans that will buy us time, so that we may advance the cause of socially responsible living, once we have gained the confidence of the people again. We have also lost the war on poverty, and the war to improve education through expanding federal influence, and the left needs to be prepared to compromise on those issues or accept the consequences of those failures.

You likely want to strangle me right now for something written in this book. It is never easy to self-analyze and we tend to look for the answers that are all too easy rather than looking deeper. We tend to hate those who point to us and say, "hey, fix this not that!" For whatever part of the overall problem I have been a part of, our fundamental failing to unite on commonalities, please accept my most humble apologies. I do want to stand with you, but we need to stop calling each other RINOs and extremists. We have got to stop yelling at each other or refusing to accept that certain candidates lost, no matter what loopholes in the rules you might find. We need to stop changing the rules at the last second to disenfranchise those who don't agree with you one hundred percent of the time.

Moreover, we cannot accept a definition of compromise that is capitulation. Democrats all but ignored Republicans prior to 2010, taking the occasional break from riding rough shot to belittle and berate us. Now, they refuse to cooperate with the Republican lead house, taking occasional breaks to belittle and berate us. In the end, we generally end up giving them what they want with few, if any concessions.

Senator Mike Lee's recent proposal to fund all functions of government, without argument, except Obamacare (for which he wants a separate vote) should not be controversial among Republicans at all. It's a more than reasonable compromise that gives Democrats most of what they want, but asks for this *one thing* in return. That Harry Reid responded by threatening to shut down the government and blaming Republicans is very telling of their attitudes toward compromise. Senator Lee's strategy has the benefit of making the Democrats *own* Obamacare, yet again. Look, funding for Obamacare will pass the house on its own. Republicans only have ten more seats than the Democrats. there's enough moderate Republicans to ensure it passes. In the Senate, however, it would have to pass on a strictly partisan vote, and while we may lose the battle, this puts us in a very good position for 2014 with the folks once angry at the Democrats for pushing through a very unpopular piece of legislation, essentially, a second time. It's brilliant. But others want to delay Obamacare. Okay, do that too, but for crying out loud, quit attacking each other and do *something*! Democrats are counting on chaos among our ranks, and if I haven't convinced you by now that our failure to stand for *something* has caused just that, as well as the continued bickering amongst ourselves causing our base to stay home, then I don't know what will. We cannot win elections if our base keeps sitting elections out. They will not show for a party without principals that is at war with itself.

Ronald Reagan once admonished us to obey the eleventh commandment, "thou shalt not speak ill of a fellow Republican." I want to be clear; I am only interested in speaking ill of those that do not follow this rule. I am only interested in replacing those, who not only berate and belittle their fellow Republicans, but actively work against the party platform. Otherwise, I am happy to stand with you.

Whether or not you agree with all of the compromises and suggestions I have included in this small volume, I hope you will agree with enough to want to pass it along. It is very important that we arrest the pendulum so we can start having the important discussions necessary to save the country. Instead, we have rampant name calling and some people looking for ways to disenfranchise the factions they don't like. I had mentioned Utah's unique caucus system. It is probably the only truly Republican system in the country, eschewing direct democracy for a representative system that grants real power to the poor and ordinary citizens. Whereas primaries are normally won by the candidate with the most money, who buries the people with attack ads, mailers, fliers and robo-calls, the caucus system almost eliminates that while enabling ordinary citizens to have a say in who the candidates will be in the first place.

Utah's counties are divided up into precincts or neighborhoods. Every two years, the neighborhood gets together and selects a delegate (maybe more than one, dependent upon the size of the precinct) a Precinct Chair, Vice Chair, Treasurer and Secretary. Now the elites in the press claim the delegates and what have you are powerful elites (basically because they are looking in the mirror), but that is far from reality. The precincts cover every neighborhood and every walk of life in Utah. In Utah someone in the area you live has a position of real power in one of either parties. You could even run if you wanted to.

The Delegate has the assignment to get to know each of the candidates and report back their findings to the neighborhood caucus participants, who then should vote on who the delegate should vote for at convention. Now to be honest, it doesn't always work this way, but when I was Precinct Chair, I saw to it that this did happen for my neighborhood.

There are problems with the caucus system, but the biggest advantage to it is that it enables ordinary citizens to run for office and succeed. That is how we landed my favorite State Senator, Daniel Thatcher, who has been among the best our state has to offer. A stalwart conservative who actually keeps his campaign promises. He's a great guy, but had no money to his name. He won by going door to door himself and building a large volunteer base to help him. It was a huge victory for the GOP when he won in a Democrat stronghold. Daniel has made himself available to his constituents and was willing to go meet the people in person. You don't have that experience in primary states. Only in Utah will a candidate for a major political party end up at your door, and furthermore only in Utah can a nobody like yours truly have candidates come to an event I organized. Yet, we've done that. We've had candidates at my house, I have interviewed them for my You Tube channel. Me, a nobody! That is the power of Utah's caucus system. Ordinary people are able to get their hands in the actual soil of the grass roots. Money has no power in Utah's politics and that is why it ought to be preserved.

Not only should it be preserved, but this last Primary was one of the nastiest Republicans have ever gone through. Ninety percent of Obama's attacks against Romney were attacks recycled from the things other Republicans said about him. You never saw the candidates meeting with individual citizens. If they went to someone's house, it was a billionaire's. Creating a national caucus based on Utah's would avoid the negative ads, would keep all that infighting out of the public eye and keep our debates *far* from the radicals at CNN and MSDNC. Individuals can then get to know each presidential candidate personally, or even have them to their home, then report back to their state or precinct or however we decide to do it. Yes, the candidates would have to work harder, but I don't see that as a bad thing. It personalizes the campaign and makes it so that the candidate is not just slinging mud at the other guy, but rather someone you can call a friend. There are many candidates, some who won, some who lost, whose friendship I value. I am proud of the work they have done and I feel I have a personal stake in that candidate or representative.

While the inter-factional fighting is at an all-time high, we as a movement must always remember we do not have the numbers to win on our own. We need each other. I have said before and will say again: only a unified Right can overcome the monumental challenges before us. Only by getting past the emotional nonsense we keep bickering over, can we ready the nation for the very real, very adult conversation we need to have: our out of control spending, debt, inflation and the impact of it all on personal liberty and civilly deposing those responsible. Stated differently, what it means for your kitchen table.

Together, there is strength and there is courage. Alone and we are destined for the ash heap of history.

Acknowledgements

I would like to thank the following people who in one way or another have shaped and influenced my political views and thought process. First to my wife Becky, who is more enthusiastic about politics than I. She is Texas' brightest star and I am so blessed to be with her. To My parents, grandparents, grandparents-in-law, and my dear friends Dan Thatcher and Sifu Steve Thatcher, thank you for teaching me and putting up with my rampant questioning of everything. To Doctor Glenn J. Kimber for introducing me to the works of Thomas Jefferson and for helping me to moderate my approach to politics. A Very special thanks to my sister-in-law, Katie Moir, for allowing me to use the picture she took of Aerith for this book. You are amazingly talented!

To Jay Brummett, Julie Dole, Gary Welch, Crystal Perry, Daniela Jones, Andres Parades, Casey Jackson, Morgan Philpot, Barbara Stallone, thank you for everything you have taught me. To Carl Wimmer, Chris Herrod and the rest of the Patrick Henry Caucus, you guys rock! I hope to see you all run for office again! To Christian Rodier, Michelle Scharf, Myranda Holgerson, Victor Shanti, Ben Soholt, Howard Wallack and the many, many, many others I have had the honor of working with over the years. I have learned so much from each of you and while we may not always agree on issues, your friendship has meant so much to me that it would be difficult to express it in writing. Thanks for everything!

ABOUT THE AUTHOR

Daniel Moir prides himself on being an average Joe-Nobody, gamer and movie fan and aspiring writer and martial artists. He has been a grass roots activist and blogger under the nick-name the Unapologetic Apologist. He has served as a Precinct Chair and Leg Chair for the Salt Lake County Republican Party, and served three years on the board of the Salt Lake County Young Republicans for whom he regularly produces videos for You Tube.

http://www.youtube.com/seraphimtheapologist
http://www.youtube.com/slcoyrs
http://seraphimtheapologist.blogspot.com/